This Week at Home:
Devotional Readings between Sundays

Joel Mark Flugstad

By the same author
Chorando por Brasil: Crônicas de um Pastor que Olhou para trás

This Week at Home:

Devotional Readings between Sundays

Joel Mark Flugstad

Lawler Street Book Concern
2014

The Scripture quotations contained herein are from the New Revised Standard
Version Bible, copyright © 1989 by the Division of Christian Education of the
National Council of the Churches of Christ in the U.S.A. Used by permission.
All rights reserved.

First Printing 2014.

ISBN 978-0-578-15476-3

Lawler Street Book Concern
Oklahoma City, OK

Contents

Preface

These short meditations were written when the author was pastor of Our Lord's Lutheran Church in Oklahoma City with the intention of encouraging daily Bible reading and prayer in the homes of the congregants, perhaps around the breakfast or dinner table. Their brevity is due to the limitations of space in the Sunday bulletin. Some have been kind enough to suggest that these short meditations could be collected in book form, which accounts for this, the first in a projected series following a three-year lectionary scheme. The perspicacious reader will note that this collection generally follows the readings assigned for Year B in the 1992 *Revised Common Lectionary*.*

The meditations have been grouped according to the seasons of the church year, but because of variations in the calendar and the movable date for Easter, no attempt has been made to assign each reading to a particular day. The urge to expand the meditations has been mostly resisted in order to preserve the succinct nature of the original project.

These readings are offered with the hope and prayer that they may edify the reader's faith in Christ Jesus.

Since only a verse, or even part of a verse, from each Bible reading is printed here, it would be valuable for the reader's devotion to have a Bible close at hand.

--jmf
Willow Creek, Oklahoma City
Saint Andrew's Day, mmxiv
"We have found the Messiah" (John 1:41)

---

*The Revised Common Lectionary, © 1992 Consultation on Common Texts.

I. Advent, Christmas and Epiphany

LORD, have mercy on all who appear before you today.
Save, O LORD, those who have no one to pray for them.
Save, O LORD, those who do not, or cannot, pray for themselves.
--Fr. Zossima, in *The Brothers Karamazov,* by Fyodor Dostoyevsky

A NEW BEGINNING
We all fade like a leaf, and our iniquities, like the wind, take us away (Isaiah 64:1-9; v. 6b).
What great joy and hope Advent brings us! It is a new beginning for a people and for a world fading away like leaves that slowly wither and fall to the ground. Now here comes the Savior Jesus, who will save us from sin, death and the power of evil. God's face, often hidden behind events that we cannot understand, is revealed and shines on us again in Jesus Christ. We need no reminders of our mortality. But Jesus is our life. *Come, Lord Jesus!*

AWESOME DEEDS
. . . you did awesome deeds that we did not expect . . . (Isaiah 64:1-9; v. 3).
God thundered from Sinai, and the mountains shook at the presence of The Almighty. As our world stumbles from one crisis to the next, we look skyward and wonder if God will intervene somehow, sometime, to save us from ourselves. So far God's answer is Jesus Christ, his death and resurrection, redemption for those who can believe it. When faith in the Son of God dawns on our consciousness, it is no less earth shaking than the moment at Sinai.

SPIRITUAL STUPOR
"Keep awake" (Mark 13:24-37; v 35).
The banner hanging on the wall of the sanctuary says "Keep Awake," startling both sleepy worshipers as well as complacent Christians. Spiritual stupor is our constant companion. A little inattention, a little feeling of boredom ("We've done this before

1

and we're doing it again"), a little distraction by the world's agenda, and spiritual stupor sets in and we are oblivious to God, to grace, to duty, to opportunity for giving glory to Jesus Christ. "Keep awake!" Jesus says. God is up to something big. We wouldn't want to miss it.

THE ENDURING WORD

"Heaven and earth will pass away, but my words will not pass away" (Mark 13:24-37; v. 31).

The physical world bears witness that everything is subject to change. Consider the formation of mountains eons ago, for example, or the receding glaciers in our day. Even the details of our life--employment, health, finances—are subject to change. What endures through it all is the Word of God, Jesus Christ, who himself is the promise of everlasting love and eternal fellowship with God.

GOD IS PRESENT

How long will you be angry with your people's prayers? (Psalm 80; v. 4).

If our prayers seem to be swallowed up by some black hole in deepest space, we should not be discouraged. It is what the Spiritual Giants of every age report. When God seems most distant it is likely that he is most present. Since our life with God depends on faith, rather than feelings, our faith is actually strongest when there seems to be no reason for believing. "My grace is sufficient for you, for power is made perfect in weakness" (2 Corinthians 12:9).

SKEPTICS AND SCOFFERS

. . . our enemies laugh among themselves . . . (Psalm 80; v.6).

The skeptic and the scoffer will always have a field day with "believers." We stake our lives on the flimsiest of structures—namely, a word, a message passed on from generation to generation. No bolts of lightning, no proofs that satisfy the scientific mind. We believe that redemption from sin and evil is available now by faith in the Lord Jesus, and we believe that this redemption will, at last, become a visible reality. Until then, scoffers will scoff and believers will believe.

STAMINA

He will also strengthen you to the end (1 Corinthians 1:3-9; v. 8). It is not only when the end nears, but all along the way we need an extra ounce or so of stamina for the spiritual life. There will always be troubles and troublers, we will always pray anxiously for daily bread, our bodies will seem to betray us, and we may wonder where God is in all our needs. We will find God on the cross, bearing all things with us, sharing with us also the power of the resurrection.

Life in a prison cell may well be compared to Advent; one waits, hopes, and does this, that or the other—things that are really of no consequence—the door is shut, and can be opened only from the outside. –Dietrich Bonhoeffer

---

A BLUE CURTAIN

O that you would tear open the heavens and come down (Isaiah 64:1-9; v.1). Enough of the hiddenness of God! Why are you so far from us? Why are you so silent? If only the curtain of the blue sky could be opened so that the glory, righteousness and justice of God could be revealed and made known, and all would know the truth of God in an instant! God is God, and God will do things according to God's purpose and will. Here the heavens are opened and we see the Child in a manger, and then on the cross. This is God's glory, righteousness, and love for this world.

THE RETURN

. . . where righteousness is at home (2 Peter 3:8-15; v. 13). Words of comfort and hope have seldom been better put. In the New Day, in God's kingdom, in the New Earth, righteousness will come home. In our world, righteousness often seems to be away on a long trip. This gives greed, hostility, suffering and idolatries of all kinds a free reign. Our longing is not for escape, but for the return of Righteousness to his home, Jesus Christ, the righteousness of God.

3

THE NEWS

Lift up your voice with strength . . . herald of good tidings . . . (Isaiah 40:1-11; v. 9).

Good tidings come from the mouth of God because the news from our lives is tough, disappointing, creating anxiety. If there is human wickedness that brings suffering, there is also divine deliverance through Jesus Christ. If there is anxiety because of human greed and irresponsibility, there is assurance from God that our needs will be satisfied. If we are disappointed by our own actions, and if the actions of others cause us distress, we hear the good tidings that God forgives us and makes us new for Jesus Christ's sake.

GETTING UNSTUCK

The beginning of the good news of Jesus Christ, the Son of God (Mark 1:1-8; v. 1).

The people were stuck. Some were obedient to unseemly behaviors because they didn't know anything else. Some were caught up in the game of getting ahead at whatever cost. Some were unable to recover from personal loss or setback. Now a herald of good tidings announces he will tell a story for everyone who is stuck: it is the story of the good news of Jesus Christ, the Son of God.

WHO NEEDS GOOD NEWS?

. . . repentance for the forgiveness of sins (Mark 1:1-8; v. 4).

It may seem strange to say that the gospel, the "good news," begins with repentance. The good news of Jesus Christ is summed up in his victory over sin, death and devil. If there were no sin, no evil, no death, neither would there be any gospel. If there is no sin, who needs good news? The first gospel step is to clasp our hands to our head and cry, "What have I done?" To which cry God sends the Savior, Jesus Christ, for forgiveness, life and salvation.

SILENCE

Let me hear what God the LORD will speak (Psalm 85; v. 8).

Silence is too much for us to bear. There is a television at home and radio in the car. There are portable devices that send music directly and exclusively into our ears. Noise of some kind is always available to us, wherever we are, so that we can avoid silence. Even in church the silence is unbearable. There is a point to Silence, however, whether at home, in the car, even in church! Silence is the place where, finally, we are alone with God. The Silence becomes bearable only because Jesus Christ is the Word of God.

THE APPOINTED TIME
Regard the patience of our Lord as salvation (2 Peter 3:8-15a; v.15a).
Maybe you are ready for Christmas, but we are never quite ready for the coming of our Lord Jesus Christ. We are distracted by concerns that belong to the old way of life, forgetting time and again that Christ has saved us from all that and made us new. Jesus will come again at God's appointed time, but the apparent delay is really a reprieve. It allows us time to examine our lives, throw out what is useless and turn in repentance to embrace God's grace in Jesus Christ.

GLORY
The glory of the LORD shall be revealed (Isaiah 40:1-11; v.5).
The brilliant sun shining in a blue sky makes one think that "It doesn't get any better than this." It will get better, when the glory of our Lord Jesus Christ is revealed, in God's good time. The ordinary sun highlights wonderful features of God's creation, both human and natural, but the sun also casts light on the problems of war, hunger, and disease. When the glory of the Lord is revealed, we will see that God has won the final victory for peace and wholeness, for us and all creation.

ANTICIPATION
May those who sow in tears reap with shouts of joy (Psalm 126; v. 5).
When tears flow it is not so easy to say, "God has done great things for us." It is usually when we are able to look back on difficulties that we can see God's gracious hand in our lives. The season of sowing is a time of anticipation. It is also a time of helplessness. When the seeds are in the ground and watered, there is nothing

more we can do. It is a time of quiet waiting. The seeds will sprout and grow in their own time. The resurrection of Jesus transforms our times of tears into seasons of hopeful anticipation, trusting that God will do great things for us yet.

IDENTITY

. . . the Jews sent priests and Levites . . .to ask [John], *"Who are you?"* (John 1:6-8, 19-28; v. 19).

Self-awareness is always a good thing. John the Baptist knew who he was and his role in the story of salvation. He was the dynamite that leveled mountains so that Jesus Christ might arrive nobly to be honored as Lord and Savior of the human race. Our identity is also connected to Jesus Christ. We are the ones he has saved from sin and death, and we are the ones who point to him as the One Who brings light into the darkness.

STRAIGHTENED OUT

Make straight the way of the Lord (John 1:19-28; v. 23).

We make our relationship with God complicated with rambling self-justifications. These are the sharp turns, the dubious forks in the road that make an honest relationship with God impossible. A straight way to the Lord is one of complete honesty, a confession of self-awareness and self-unawareness. Along this straight path, suddenly we look up and it is the Lord Jesus himself coming to straighten us out.

THE RIGHT CLOTHING

. . . the LORD . . . has clothed me with the garments of salvation (Isaiah 61:8-11; v. 10).

What we could not do for ourselves God does for us. We cannot contrive to cover over our unworthiness, no matter how stylish or trendy we think we are. The Lord Jesus takes our unworthiness into himself, and clothes us with his righteousness. Laying aside the works of darkness, we have put on Christ, as the apostle says (Romans 13:14). Transformation into Christ-likeness is not by dressing ourselves with outward piety but by believing that the gift of righteousness really is for us.

6

INTO HUMAN FLESH
The Lord is with you (Luke 1:26-38; v. 28).

With Mary we wonder what sort of greeting is this? Out of the blue, without any warning, without any urging on our part, whether we feel sinful or righteous, whether we were waiting for it or not, the Lord God comes into our lives. In Jesus God has not only entered into human history but into human flesh as well. The long separation from God is over. "Let it be to me according to your word!"

PONDERING
She was much perplexed . . . and pondered (Luke 1:26-38; v. 29).

What does it mean that Jesus wants to be born into my life? We could rush around with the crowds and run away from the question. Or, we could sit quietly in silence and ponder with Mary, and never fully understand or appreciate the mystery of 'Christ in us.' *O holy child of Bethlehem / Descend to us we pray / Cast out our sin and enter in / Be born in us today.* (Phillips Brooks, 1835-1893)

BREATHLESS
Do not be afraid, Mary (Luke 1:26-38; v. 30).

When God comes into our lives, suddenly, it is surely an event worthy of fear and trembling. The God of heaven and earth cares about you! Run away and hide, if you feel like it—God will come after you. In the end, breathless from flight, we discover that God has pursued us that we may be "highly favored" in the love of Jesus Christ.

INTIMACY WITH GOD
. . . the power of the Most High will overshadow you (Luke 1:26-38; v. 35).

This is what we most desire and most fear. We fear intimacy with God because we will be changed. Something unpredictable will happen to us. Ask Mary! Maybe we will love our enemy. Maybe we will give up an obsession or a resentment. That is the power of the Host High. We fear it, but we also desire it because we know life cannot go on like this!

LET IT BE!
Then Mary said, "Here am I, the servant of the Lord; let it be with me according to your word" (Luke 1:26-38; v. 38).

A man visiting a monastery just before Christmas met a monk on the sidewalk. The man greeted the monk, saying, "Merry Christmas." The monk replied, "May Christ be born in you." Jesus wants to be born in us, and may we, with Mary, say, "Let it be!"

THE MIGHTY ONE
The Mighty One has done great things for me (Luke 1:46b-55; v.49).

Blessed Mary carries in her womb the Savior of the world. The great things of God are beyond her imagination and ours. Through Mary's Child the Mighty One not only forgives our sins but works in us to transform desires and attitudes The Mighty One takes up residence in our hearts and lives, surprising us when conflicts are resolved. The great things of God are still reserved for us on the Day of Resurrection, when we will be transformed beyond imagination.

ABRAHAM'S OFFSPRING
. . . to Abraham and his descendants forever (Luke 1:46b-55; v. 55).

Abraham could not have foreseen, even with a vivid imagination, how God's promises would be fulfilled. When we cannot see or imagine, which is most of the time, we live by faith. Those who live by faith in Christ Jesus are Abraham's offspring. In the midst of turmoil and uncertainty, guilt and doubt, what sustains us is the promise that God will love us, redeem us, forgive us through the grace of the Lord Jesus. Those who can believe this are Abraham's children, heirs of God's promises.

THE WILL OF GOD (PART I)
Rejoice always . . . for this is the will of God in Christ Jesus for you (1 Thessalonians 5:16-24; vv. 16, 18).

Outward circumstances often make rejoicing seem inappropriate. Sometimes the imperative 'Rejoice!' sounds more like law than grace. The key is "in Christ Jesus"—the will of God *in Christ*

Jesus. "In Christ Jesus" changes everything. Out rejoicing is not *because* of circumstances but because of the *new circumstance* of being "in Christ," bound with him in victory, in love, in grace and power to make the new creation come alive in us.

THE WILL OF GOD (PART II)

Pray without ceasing . . . for this is the will of God in Christ Jesus for you (1 Thessalonians 5:16-24; vv. 17, 18).

 Our spiritual welfare depends on the constant presence of the Spirit of God in our lives. It is "God's will in Christ Jesus" that we should be infused with the Spirit in such a way that prayer is as automatic as breathing. So begin by praying simply "Jesus" as you breathe in and out. You will discover that "in Christ Jesus" God's Spirit prays in us and with us and for us.

THE WILL OF GOD (PART III)

Give thanks in all circumstances; for this is the will of God in Christ Jesus for you (1 Thessalonians 5:16-24; v. 18).

Rejoicing, praying, giving thanks are all of a piece, aspects of the same attitude that being "in Christ Jesus" creates in us. There is plenty of room in our prayers for complaints, but complaints and needs of all kinds are offered up in the context of thanksgiving for all God has done and promised in Jesus Christ.

THE SAVIOR IS BORN

. . . the time came . . . (Luke 2:1-20; v. 6).

Scheduled C-sections and other modern procedures notwithstanding, babies are born at the right time. There is a period of waiting, planning, hoping, wondering. Then it happens. So it is with God's plans and purposes. A Savior is promised; hope is generated; expectations are formed; then in God's own time it happens. The Savior, Christ the Lord, is born. Wonderfully Son of Mary and Son of God, human and divine. The One who saves the world from sin and death is none other than the Lord of heaven and earth. The time has come for Jesus to be born in us, to let our lives take the shape of his life.

ADVENT, CHRISTMAS AND EPIPHANY
HEAVEN AND NATURE SING
O sing to the LORD a new song (Psalm 98; 1).
Seldom noted, but *Joy to the World,* the Christmas hymn of Isaac
Watts (1674-1748) is actually a paraphrase of Psalm 98. "Heaven
and nature sing" will find its echo in the verses of this psalm. "Let
the sea roar . . . Let the floods clap their hands . . . at the presence
of the LORD." Very often we prefer old songs to new songs. "Joy
to the World" was once a new song, and even continues to be both
new and renewing as we contemplate "the wonders of his love"
each Christmas season.

GOD-IN-THE-FLESH
The Word became flesh (John 1:1-14; v. 14).
Prophets, sages, gurus and inspirational leaders of every kind
encourage us in our spiritual development toward more
compassion and more love. Easy for them to say! We wear
ourselves out trying. On the other hand Jesus—God-in-the-flesh,
fully divine and fully human—does not nag us into righteousness,
but becomes "cursed" for our sake in order to make us righteous,
blessed, and compassionate. The hope of reconciling humanity and
opening the door to life with God now and forever does not depend
on us but centers in God's Word made flesh, Jesus Christ.

*The most precious is Christ himself, but the next precious is to
have a martyr's mind, the Christian martyr's mind. With this
mind we once conquered the world, and without it the world will
conquer us.* –Kaj Munk (1898-1944)

ST. STEPHEN, DEACON AND MARTYR
"I send you prophets . . . some of whom you will kill" (Matthew
23:34-39; v. 34).
Followers of Jesus will discover that the way of discipleship is also
the way of the cross. Stephen was the first to experience, in his
flesh, what it means to be a Christian. He also shows us the
meaning of discipleship when, taught by the Lord himself, he
prays, "Lord, do not hold this sin against them" (Acts 7:60). When
our discipleship comes to an end, Stephen teaches us to pray, "Lord
Jesus, receive my spirit" (Acts 7:59).

10

ST. JOHN, APOSTLE AND EVANGELIST

... the world ... could not contain the books ... (John 21:20-25; v. 25).

A well-known atheist was asked, "Suppose you die and actually see God. What would you say? He answered, "Not enough evidence, Lord!" Unfaith always asks for more—more signs, more proof, more convincing arguments. Faith hears the word of Jesus and believes. What we need to know about Jesus is written in the witness of John and the other evangelists. John's testimony is that "God so loved the world that he gave his only begotten Son . . ." This was written so that we might believe.

THE HOLY INNOCENTS, MARTYRS

Out of Egypt I have called my Son (Matthew 2:13-18; v. 15).

With all the warmth, good cheer, and friendliness all around us at Christmas, it is jarring to be reminded of the reason for Jesus' birth and incarnation. Jesus is, after all the Savior, who came to save the world from cold, heartless, and inhumane actions. Even as the Christmas spirit fades away, we proclaim with joy: Christ the Savior is born!

SIMEON

Simeon ... righteous and devout ... the Holy Spirit rested on him (Luke 2:22-35; v. 25).

In his lifetime Simeon could have built skyscrapers or bridges, for all we know, but Scripture tells us only that he was righteous and devout, and full of the Holy Spirit. Nothing more needs to be said about Simeon, or about us. Jesus Christ makes us righteous and gives us the Holy Spirit. We seek both to be devoted to Christ as well as to the company of the devout who serve the Lord Jesus. Then whatever is "done" arises from the Spirit of Christ within. *Glory to you, O Christ!*

ANNA

Anna ... never left the temple but worshiped there with fasting and prayer night and day (Luke 2:36-40; v. 37).

What a bundle of energy Anna must have been! At the age of 84, fasting and praying. Didn't she get hungry or tired? The hungry

11

and tired ones were those "who were looking for the redemption of Jerusalem." Anna, full of energy, rushed to tell the good news. "God has redeemed us from our burdens!" No time for weariness or hunger here. So much to tell to so many people! *Praise to You, O Christ!*

THE NAME
. . . at the name of Jesus . . . (Philippians 2:5-11; v. 10).
Our salvation has a name. It is Jesus. The love of God for the human race has a name: Jesus. The beginning and end of one revolution around the sun, and the beginning and end of all things has a name: Jesus. Our hope for bringing enemies together in peace has a name: Jesus. Release from our own individual captivities has a name: Jesus. The One through whom God will accomplish his plans and purpose for everything created has a name. It is Jesus Christ, our Lord.

NEW YEAR
. . . the Lord make his face to shine upon you . . . (Numbers 6:22-27; v. 25).
This is our prayer, hope and God's promise for each of us at the beginning of a new year, as time is measured. The promise is that when we leave time and enter eternity the face of God will shine on us perpetually, so that we will need no other light. Our hope and prayer for each other is that, in this life as well, we may live courageously, with our path illuminated by the face of God that has been revealed to us, Jesus Christ our Lord.

PARANOID TYRANTS
King Herod . . . was frightened . . . (Matthew 2:1-12; v. 3).
Such a tiny creature, lodged in a small town, but accompanied by such intriguing portents. The visitors from a far country know something that Herod does not. Tyrants are paranoid with good reason. Their power always teeters on the edge. Now comes King Jesus with the power of grace, and forgiveness, the power even over death and evil. "Let this world's tyrant rage," says the hymn. God's Word will prevail, and those who feared the oppression of sin and evil fear no more.

URGENT WORDS

Search diligently for the child (Matthew 2:1-12; v. 8).

No political leader ever spoke more urgent words: search diligently for Christ. He is your light, your life, your hope of seeing God face to face. Christ is your peace, your courage in the face of evil, your reason for living. Bound up in Christ Jesus you are freed from whatever it is in your life that enslaves.

GUIDED TO JESUS

When they saw that the star had stopped, they were overwhelmed with joy (Matthew 2:1-12; v. 10).

They had come a long way, and so have we. Bouncing along on dusty roads, they are guided to Jesus. Through disappointments and anxieties, by way of opportunities seized or missed, the paths of our lives have brought us to this time and place. God's Spirit has brought us face to face with Jesus Christ, the Savior from all that afflicts body or soul. The longer we have been searching the greater the joy. The longer we have lived in the Presence without knowing it, the greater the joy when we discover it.

OUR BEST

Then, opening their treasure chests they offered him gifts of gold, frankincense and myrrh (Matthew 2:1-12; v. 11).

They come bearing kingly gifts for the King of kings. Only the best is good enough for Jesus. Whatever our 'best' is it will be in accord with what we have to work with, not in comparison with anyone else. Let the magi offer to Jesus according to their means and ability. Our offering will be in response to the call of God to let Jesus be the Sovereign Ruler of our lives, and to give him the best of our time, talents and treasure.

A GREATER LOYALTY

May all kings fall down before him, all nations give him service (Psalm 72; v. 11).

Obedience to our local laws and rulers is important for the sake of order in society and for the well-being of our neighbor. There is, however, a greater loyalty and obedience owed to Jesus, the King

13

of kings and Lord of lords. The royal Rule of Jesus is to end suspicion, mistrust, and enmity among the peoples. All who lead nations, organizations or households bow down before the One whom God has named Sovereign Lord of this world, Jesus Christ.

AN OPEN SECRET

. . . so that through the church the wisdom of God . . . might now be made known . . . (Ephesians 3:1-12; v. 10).

There is nothing like a mystery to get our attention, and nothing like a mystery revealed to make a story with a satisfying ending. The church has a story to tell, a mystery that is no longer hidden, an 'open secret.' God's plan and purpose for our world is to bring all people into the grace of the Lord Jesus. We are the church for the purpose of telling God's story.

THE SON OF GOD

"You are my Son" (Mark 1:4-11; v. 11).

The Son of God has thrown his lot in with the human race. Our fate is his fate, down to the final terror of death. We cling by faith to Christ who has transformed our fate from a hopeless situation into a victory, so that just as he took our weakness into himself, he gives us the victory of his resurrection and the promise of the glory of his exaltation.

GOD SPEAKS

Then God said . . . (Genesis 1:1-5; v. 3).

Noise pollution is a thoroughly modern complaint. Quietly, in the background, comes the voice of God. If our hearts and minds are tuned in it can be clearly heard above the din of electronic beeps and howls. God's will and purpose are carried out by his word. God declares, and there is light; God speaks, and there is order out of chaos, something out of nothingness. Now, God has spoken in a unique way, through his Son! It is Jesus, God's word in the flesh, who calls us into light, who puts order into the chaos of our lives, and who makes us completely alive.

THE VOICE

. . . the voice of the Lord breaks the cedars (Psalm 29; v. 5).

When the wind blows gently to cool us on a summer day, we are willing to say this is the voice of God. Sometimes the signs are too powerful for us to make sense of. When the wind breaks the cedars and whirls oak trees around, we are less willing to hear in this the voice of God. In the end, when all is still again, there is another voice, Christ, the Word of God, who is for us God's shalom, our perfect peace.

GLORY!

. . . and in his temple all say, "Glory!" (Psalm 29; v. 9).

The Glorious Presence of the Creator of All Things, the God of the Universe, now fills our world, our temple, our homes and lives through the Presence of Jesus Christ. The glory of God is seen at the River Jordan where the Son of God is not ashamed to stand in line with sinners. God's glory is revealed in Jesus' works of healing, compassion, forgiveness of sins. God's glory is revealed chiefly in the death and resurrection of Jesus, the victory over sin and death. When we look to Jesus we behold the glory of God.

A BURNING FLAME

He will baptize you with the Holy Spirit (Mark 1:4-11; v. 8).

Baptism into Christ *is* baptism of the Holy Spirit. We should not doubt for a minute that we are "in the Spirit." If we believe in Christ it is a sign that the flame of the Spirit already burns within us. Perhaps it is a small flame, but it burns nevertheless. We should not be afraid to let the Spirit of our Lord Jesus Christ turn up the heat, if that is God's will for us.

LIFE CHANGING RESULTS

"We have not even heard that there is a Holy Spirit" (Acts 19:1-7; v. 2).

It is possible that there are believers in Christ who are unaware of the Holy Spirit. The Spirit draws our attention to Christ, and as we focus on Christ it is possible to overlook the work of the Spirit. "Strive for the spiritual gifts" (1 Corinthians 14:1), says the Apostle, for the Spirit of Christ brings about life changing results

15

in our lives. Paul names some of them: "Love, joy, peace, patience, kindness . . ." (Galatians 5:22). Then, at the last, "life to your mortal bodies also through his Spirit that dwells in you" (Romans 8:11).

NOTHING ELSE MATTERS

"Follow me" (John 1:43-51; v. 43).

There is great economy in the call of our Lord. There is no pleading, no attempt to explain the benefits of discipleship. He says simply, Follow me. Jesus is not selling us a product that may fill a perceived need. Jesus is exercising his absolute lordship over us. There is no claim that can compete with the claim of Jesus. Follow me. Nothing else matters.

NEEDING CHRIST

"Come and see" (John 1:43-51; v. 46).

Our witness points to Christ: people do not need us, they need Christ. Christ will deal with them according to God's will and purpose, just as Christ has dealt with us in our own unique condition. You might have an interesting story to tell, and there may be times to tell it. But we want to point people to Jesus, not to ourselves. "I want to know Christ!" (Philippians 3:10). We have found the Promised One. Come and see.

THE INCESSANT GAZE

Even before a word is on my tongue, O LORD you know it (Psalm 139; v. 4).

There is no hiding from God. Not even in our deepest, most secret thoughts, can we escape God's notice. The incessant gaze of God ultimately is for blessing, not ill. God is interested in us. God wants us to acknowledge that our lives pass under the judgment and grace of God. If our Lord knows everything about us, it is to deliver us from the things that harm us, and to bring us into a place of blessing.

GREATER THINGS
"Do you believe because I told you I saw you under the fig tree?"
(John 1:43-51; v. 50).

There is a frisson of terror when we remember that God sees us under the fig tree and everywhere else besides. It might drive us to a kind of fearful acknowledgement of God's omnipotence, but not necessarily to a loving trust in God's goodness. "Greater things" are on the way for the disciples of Jesus Christ. The One who sees us brings light and life, love and joy into our fearful, trembling, darkened hearts. The Lamb of God who takes away the sin of the world embraces us into fellowship with the Father who sees all and loves us still.

THE BODY OF CHRIST
Therefore, glorify God in your [pl.] *body* (1 Corinthians 6:12-20; v. 5).

There are bodies and there is the one Body, the Body of Christ. Individually (each body) we are members of the one Body. Of course, as persons redeemed by the precious blood of Christ, we are to take care of our individual bodies. We also care for The Body, for each other, through love, forgiveness, compassion, and patience. When these things happen, God is glorified.

CHANGE OF ATTITUDE
"Repent" (Mark 1:14-20; v. 15).

To repent is to adjust one's attitude, and we need to do this every day. When we encounter success, we become proud and forget about God. When we make mistakes we try to cover up or deny or blame. If our life is neither good nor bad, just dull, it is because we have become insensitive to God's presence. Here is the secret that changes our attitude and unlocks the desire to do it: confession always occurs in the context of the grace of God in Jesus Christ.

GOOD NEWS
Believe in the good news (Mark 1:14-20; v. 15).

To be saved is to recognize that we have received something from God that we did not earn or acquire on our own. The good news (gospel) is that God forgives our sins and covers us with the righteousness of Christ. We stand in the presence of God without fear, not because we are pretty good or good enough, but because Christ has placed us here. That is what we have received, and that is what we believe.

POURING IT ALL OUT
Pour out your heart before him (Psalm 62; v. 8).
It is a joy and comfort to find a friend in whom we can confide with absolute confidence. We can brag about how well things are going for us with anyone. But it is only with a true friend that we can disclose our anxieties and deepest fears. The cross of Christ invites us to pour out everything to God, who comforts us beyond telling.

HOLDING EVERYTHING TOGETHER
The present form of this world is passing away (1 Corinthians 7:29-31; v. 31).
The first Christians thought they might also be the last. After all these years, God's Spirit instills in us a lively hope for the day of Jesus Christ. This hope puts all things in perspective. Neither people, nor things, nor institutions last forever. In a world whose form is "passing away" what holds us and everything else together is Jesus Christ.

GOING FISHING
"I will make you fish for people" (Mark 1:14-20; v. 17).
There was a boy in high school who played basketball and was quite good. One day he told his coach he was giving up basketball in order to "witness for Christ." The coach told the team that he let him go "because I know he'll actually do it." Many Christians feel bad because they would like to fish for people but don't know what to do if they caught one. Whatever 'witness' may mean for each one of us, it is Jesus who will teach us all we need to know.

SELF-AUTHENTICATING POWER
He taught them as one having authority (Mark 1:21-28; v. 22).
Some prophets seem worth listening to and others are merely loud voices shouting aimlessly in the plaza. When Jesus speaks his

words carry self-authenticating power to do what they proclaim. The legitimate word of God will draw our hearts and minds to Christ Jesus. Other voices in the religious marketplace are alluring, making us feel good. Some give 'practical' advice for successful living. Among the competing voices only words that proclaim Christ for us can be counted as 'Word of God.'

CLEAN SPIRITS
He commands even the unclean spirits (Mark 1:21-29; v. 27).
This Child born of Mary in the little town of Bethlehem, raised in Galilee, far from the centers of influence and power, now comes to be revealed as the One to whom "All authority in heaven and on earth" has been given. This authority extends even to unclean spirits. Whatever is unclean or unworthy in our hearts and lives is driven away by the command of Jesus.

BOWING DOWN
There are many gods and many lords (1 Corinthians 8:1-13; v. 5).
There are many interests and many important things in life. There are duties and responsibilities that demand our time and energy. We need to continually check to see what, or Who, is at the center. Martin Luther put it this way: *"That to which your heart clings and entrusts itself is, I say, really your God."* The First Commandment, Luther says, is God's way of saying, *"Whatever good thing you lack, look to me for it and seek it from me, and whenever you suffer misfortune and distress, come and cling to me. I am the one who will satisfy you and help you out of every need. Only let your heart cling to no one else."**

---

*Luther's "Large Catechism," in *Book of Concord.* Ed. Theodore G. Tappert. © 1959 Fortress Press. P. 365.

EATING MEAT
Some have become accustomed to idols (1 Corinthians 8:1-13; v. 7).
The question of eating meat sacrificed to idols seems irrelevant 2000 years later. Nevertheless the question of idols will not go away. Whatever it is we place our trust in, Luther says, *is* our god.

It is not meat that we sacrifice, but we do make sacrifices to accommodate *something* in the center of our lives. It might be a struggle to keep Christ at the center. Worse than the struggle, however, is to become accustomed to finding Christ on the periphery.

A TRUE PROPHET

. . . a prophet who presumes to speak . . . a word that I have not commanded (Deuteronomy 18:15-20; v. 20).

How are we to know the true prophet from the false prophet? One indication is reluctance. The true prophets go forth reluctantly, struggling with the Call from God, while the false prophets often seem too eager, thirsty for success. Another indication is the content of the prophet's message. Paul proclaimed "Christ and him crucified." The genuine prophet will echo that message.

COVENANT

He is ever mindful of his covenant (Psalm 111; v. 5).

There is a tie that binds even closer and tighter than the bond between loving Christians. It is the bond of God's covenant with us established in Jesus Christ through holy Baptism. Here God promises to free us from the triple threat of sin, death and evil. At the same time God calls us to faith, i.e., to believe that God really does this for us. From time to time we may forget that we are in this covenant relationship with God. God however, is ever mindful of his covenant.

IN TOWN

The whole city was gathered together at the door (Mark 1:29-39; v. 33).

When the word goes out that the One who bears our infirmities and carries our diseases (Isaiah 53) is in town, it will not be long before the whole city gathers at the door. The healing Jesus brings may or may not be physical, but it is always a healing of the rift between God and us. We entrust all who are ill to God's care, praying for their recovery. Christ brings healing that goes beyond the cure.

DEMONS
He cast out many demons . . . he went . . . casting out demons (Mark 1:29-39; vv. 34, 39).
There are some things that are beyond scientific classification. Jesus did not scoff at the idea that people could be tormented by demons. The power of God revealed in Jesus Christ was such that the forces arrayed against God and against God's people recognized Jesus as God's Holy One and acknowledged His Power over them. When that dark cloud gathers to vex our spirits it is the Name of Jesus that dispels the danger and brings calm to troubled souls.

BEYOND WORDS
He heals the broken hearted (Psalm 147; v. 3).
A broken bone can be set, and it will heal. A cut on the finger can be washed and bandaged and it will soon be as good as new. But how do you heal a heart when it breaks? There are times when words are useless. Friends sit in silence with us. They venture a word or two, but nothing helps. Then we turn the pain and anguish over to our Lord Jesus Christ and we discover healing that goes beyond words.

WAITING
. . . those who wait for the LORD shall renew their strength (Isaiah 40:27-31; v. 31).
When we finally become energized for action we rush right in, unaware of the words of Jesus to the post-resurrection community of believers: "Wait here for the promise of the Father," i.e., the Holy Spirit. Our prayers tend to be filled with our words, imploring God to do this or that, asking God to approve our plans. Then we turn off the switch and miss out on the best part, namely, the sweet silence filled with the Presence of God's Spirit. "Those who wait" find an energy that does not come from us.

THE IMPETUS AND GOAL
I do it all for the sake of the gospel (1 Corinthians 9:16-23; v. 23). In Christ our lives are not our own. We belong to God's new creation, and everything follows from that. It influences our relationship with spouse, children and co-workers. However and wherever God leads us as Christians, the impetus and goal is the life giving death and resurrection of Jesus Christ.

BOUND TO CHRIST, I AM FREE
. . . under Christ's law (1 Corinthians 9:16-23; v. 21). Christ has freed me from my obsessions and oppressions and now I belong to him. Sin has no power over me because I belong to Christ. Death no longer intimidates, because I belong to Christ, the Resurrection and the Life. Since the Name of Jesus is connected to my name by baptism, "I fear no evil" (Psalm 23). Bound to Christ, I am free to love God with all my heart and to love my neighbor as myself. The law of Christ is perfect freedom.

OBEDIENCE
Go, wash . . . and be clean (2 Kings 5:9-14; v. 10). There is an aspect of faith that is not always visible, namely the response of obedience, 'the obedience of faith' (Romans 1:5). Does God really transform my life? Does God really lead me out of misplaced priorities into the lordship of Jesus Christ? The only way to find out is to get up and Go! You will see that Christ Jesus frees you from all that weighs you down. Let Jesus rule in your heart and life and you will discover the Newness.

GOD'S WILL
"I do choose. Be made clean!" (Mark 1:40-45; v. 41). The clear will of God is on the side of health, cleansing, restoration to community life, fellowship with God. The will of God is expressed in Jesus Christ. Whatever keeps us from enjoying the life God has given us stirs God to action. God's will is to make us clean, and the power that accomplishes this takes place in Jesus' word and command to us.

IT IS DONE

"Be made clean!" (Mark 1:40-45; v. 41).

The power of the Lord Jesus is highly economical. With three words in English, just one in Greek, it is done! When Jesus, moved with pity, sees our need, he says a word and we are cleansed, forgiven, restored, comforted, defended. It all begins with the recognition of our need and God's power to do what we cannot do for ourselves. Honesty, that vulnerable openness before God, will enable us to know the fullness of God's power and love for us. As at the beginning, God speaks and it is done and ever shall be.

SOMETHING TO SAY

"Say nothing to anyone" (Mark 1:40-45; v. 44).

On the one hand this command of Jesus is easy to keep. It is easier for us to say nothing than something, because if we were commanded to say something, what would we say? Jesus cured the sick, but did not want *that* to be the heart and soul of the Christian message. After his death and resurrection, he commanded us to "Go, make disciples." It is Christ's healing and life giving power on the cross that is to be made known.

WITNESS

He went out and began to proclaim it freely (Mark 1:40-45; v. 45).

Witness is not about technique or mechanics. In fact, against the advice of Jesus the man was telling everyone what Jesus had done for hm. If we think we "need help," or need "a program" for witness, it may simply mean that we are unaware of the depth and breadth of God's grace for us in Jesus Christ. Evangelism begins within. Look to yourself and see what Jesus has done, or still is able to do! The first witness is to oneself.

YES!

In him every one of God's promises is a "Yes" (2 Corinthians 1:18-22; v. 20).

Everyone who reads the Bible has a method for understanding or interpreting Scripture. Let us be clear about our method. We understand that the Word of God is Jesus. The Bible is God's Word because it points us to Jesus. The Bible is not a puzzle to be pieced together by clever experts, but a fully woven tapestry with Christ as theme and focus. Whether looking forward from the perspective of the Old Testament, or looking forward from where we sit, God's promises of love and redemption all find their fulfillment in Jesus.

GOD FORGIVES OUR SINS

Who can forgive sins but God alone? (Mark 2:1-12; v. 7).
And who can determine the criteria for forgiveness, but God alone? In that moment, under the retractable roof of someone's house, God was present in Jesus who declared, "Your sins are forgiven." God has determined that, on account of the death and resurrection of Jesus, sins will be forgiven. Daily we turn to God in repentance, and daily we rejoice that, for Jesus' sake, God forgives our sins!

SERVE, IN THE NAME OF CHRIST

Happy are those who consider the poor (Psalm 41; v. 1).
This psalmist is worried about people who will gloat over the poet's misfortune. "My enemies wonder in malice when I will die . . ." (v. 5). Let us be confident that God does not share the point of view that someone's illness or weakness or need is a judgment or a reason for others to rejoice. Our own need helps us to turn to God in faith. The neediness of other people offers us a chance to serve them, in the name of Christ.

HOMECOMING

I am about to do a new thing (Isaiah 43:18-25; v. 19).
There are hints along the way about God's new thing. The despair of Exile turns into a homecoming with shouts of joy (see Psalm 126, for example). The earlier call to Abraham now becomes a call to "all the ends of the earth" (Isaiah 45:22). These are clues that God has something in mind bigger than we can imagine. Deliverance from sin and death and the ingathering of the nations is promised through Jesus Christ. How God will bring this to fulfillment will undoubtedly surprise us. Perhaps God has a role for us in this?

PURE AS SNOW

I am he who blots out your transgressions for my own sake (Isaiah 43:18-25; v.25).

If it were God's desire to bring judgment upon a sinful humanity, the Son of God would not have become incarnate and the cross would not have occurred. "For my sake" I blot out transgressions, says the Lord of hosts. God's desire is to bring us all into his glorious presence, cleansed of sin, pure as the driven snow (Isaiah 1:18). The God we worship through Jesus Christ would rather forgive than condemn, even if it means the crucifixion of God's Son to make it happen.

UNCIVIL LIFE

I will abolish the bow, the sword, and war from the land (Hosea 2:14-20; v. 18).

When we are not in a right relationship with God, people around us suffer the consequences. Family life deteriorates, it becomes hard to maintain positive interactions with other people, and the civil life becomes uncivil. In our world where the bow and sword are still brandished we pray for all people to be reconciled to God and to each other. God's plan is to bring all people under the rule of Christ in a kingdom where bow and sword are no longer needed.

LIFE IN THE SPIRIT

. . . the letter kills, but the Spirit gives life (2 Corinthians 3:1-6; v. 6).

The Law is rigorous and allows for no exceptions. The Law shows us our sin and our need for God. The Spirit brings us to faith in Christ. The Spirit convinces us that we are forgiven, that we belong to the fellowship of God's people and that even when death calls, what awaits us is "the resurrection of the body and the life everlasting."

A GLORIOUS REALITY

. . . as far as the east is from the west . . . (Psalm 103:1-13; v. 12).

If sin is the grim reality about human life, forgiveness in the name of Jesus Christ is the glorious reality of life ruled by the gospel.

Sins are really forgiven and taken away, far away. How far? As far the east is from the west!

CALLED TO BE FORGIVEN

"I have come to call not the righteous, but sinners" (Mark 2:13-22; v. 17).

Grace is meaningless if you do not consider yourself a sinner. If you believe you are a righteous person, good for you. You are on your own. Christ can do nothing for you. If, however, you sense somehow that you have sinned and your life falls short of the glory of God (Romans 3:23), then there is good news: Christ calls *you*, to be forgiven, renewed and restored to perfect fellowship with God.

FRESH WINESKINS

"One puts new wine into fresh wineskins" (Mark 2:13-22; v. 22).

Fresh wineskins are always troubling for traditional Christians. Our traditions and customs, our songs and activities are comfortable and we resist changing the old for the fresh. The gospel is always new wine, and the new wine is always changing us, unless we are indifferent and unmoved by God's grace. We ourselves are the vessels in which the gospel is communicated to the world. Let the new wine bring a sparkle to your life!

TRANSFIGURATION

Six days later . . . he was transfigured before them (Mark 9:2-9; v. 2).

The Transfiguration of Jesus, as an event, does not stand alone. It only makes sense when looking back and forward. "Quite openly," the evangelist says, Jesus announced "he must undergo suffering and death" (Mark 8:31). And on the way down from the mountain he instructs his disciples not to talk about the experience until after his resurrection. The One on the cross, having taken upon himself the sin, suffering, and even the death of the human race, is revealed on the mountain as God's Son!

OUR EXPERIENCE WITH JESUS

Tell no one . . . until after the Son of Man had risen from the dead
(Mark 9:2-9; v. 9).

There is a time and a place to talk about our experience with Jesus
Christ. If we allow ourselves to be open to the Spirit's' guidance,
we will discern when and where and how to speak. Jesus often
cautioned people to "tell no one" because there is always the
possibility of bearing witness to the wrong things. Our message,
after all, is Jesus Christ. It is not our experience as such but our
experience of the cross and resurrection of Jesus that forms the
content of our witness.

A VEIL, A BLINDFOLD, AND A MASK

The god of this world has blinded the minds of the unbelievers (2
Corinthians 4:3-6; v. 4).

On the one hand there is the gospel, veiled except to the eyes of
faith. On the other hand, unbelievers are blindfolded by "the god
of this world" who in turn is masked by trendy appeals to our worst
instincts. Shining through the veil the glory of God in Jesus Christ
finds its way into the dark corners of this world to unmask evil and
rescue the perishing. We and all who have been rescued in this
fashion marvel at the reach of God's grace.

LORDSHIP

We proclaim Jesus Christ as Lord (2 Corinthians 4:3-6; v. 5).

The concept of 'lordship' sounds medieval to our modern ears. We
prefer to be colleagues, partners, associates—a team! Nevertheless
we acknowledge Jesus as Lord. We bend and shape our wills to
conform to Christ's will. We identify ourselves with his life of
service, sacrifice, self-denial and obedience, trusting that this is the
Way that leads to Life.

THE FACE OF JESUS

God . . . said, 'Let light shine out of darkness (2 Corinthians 4:3-
6; v. 6).

When children die tragically in a classroom or when a mother gives
birth in a tree in flooded Mozambique we search frantically for a
hopeful ray of light. The light coming from the face of Jesus not

only gives power to reassemble broken lives, but also points us to those whose need is infinitely greater than our own. We offer aid and comfort in Jesus' name.

THE DARK CORNERS

God . . . has shone in our hearts (2 Corinthians 4:3-6; v. 6).

It is remarkable and beyond all understanding that somehow the light of the gospel of Jesus Christ has illumined all the dark corners of our souls. What we tried to hide from God, even the things we have tried to hide from ourselves, have been revealed and sent scurrying away by the bright light of Jesus Christ. The light of Christ reveals selfishness, resentment, jealousy, and everything else that flourishes in the dark. In its place there is the joy of Jesus' presence, and love for God and neighbor.

28

II. Lent

THE JESUS PRAYER

Lord Jesus Christ,
Son of God,
have mercy upon me,
a sinner.

[This is a 'breath prayer,' prayed more or less 'without ceasing' under one's breath. At times it may be coordinated with one's breathing, according to circumstance and need. It may also be abbreviated as needed.]

ASH WEDNESDAY
You desire truth in the inward being; therefore teach me wisdom in my secret heart (Psalm 51; v. 6).
The smudge of ashes on the forehead is meant to be an aid to help us find the truth in our inner being. When we remember that we are dust, and to dust we shall return, pride and arrogance leave us and we stand empty before God. No power over our own span of life, no righteousness to boast of. *We* have nothing; by faith in Jesus Christ God gives us *all things*.

STANDING IN LINE
. . . the Beloved . . . (Mark 1:9-15; v. 11).
Now there stands Jesus, God's Son, in line with sinners at John's baptismal campout, and the Father's voice, "I love you." That the Son of God became incarnate (in the flesh) is remarkable in itself. That he was born a human to die a human death stretches the limits of our comprehension. In the Father's love for the Son we glimpse the Father's love for us. God gave the Beloved Son in sacrifice for our sake. God so loved the world.

29

TEMPTATION

The Spirit immediately drove him out into the wilderness (Mark 1:9-15; v. 12).

Things take an abrupt turn. A thrilling voice from heaven one moment, temptation in the wilderness the next. On the mountain top with an intense experience of Jesus, then suddenly we are in the valley where there is no sign of ecstasy. "No blessing goes unchallenged," some people say. If our sense of God's Presence fluctuates wildly from moment to moment we should not be alarmed. It is not the experience that is important but trust in God's word. In the wilderness, whether of distress or temptation, we are not alone. The Beloved Son is with us.

COVENANT

I am establishing my covenant with you (Genesis 9:8-17; v. 9).

"Covenant" is a good biblical word, useful for building up our faith. Covenant is commitment. God's commitment to Noah to safeguard the human race from destruction is renewed in Jesus Christ. We are brought into this covenant through baptism. "I will remember my covenant" (v. 15), is God's promise to us. *"His oath, his covenant . . . sustain me in the raging flood . . . On Christ, the solid rock, I stand; all other ground is sinking sand."* (--Edward Mote, 1787-1874)

THE RAINBOW

"I will see [my bow] and remember the everlasting covenant" (Genesis 9:8-17; v. 16).

It has always been God's intention to save, not to destroy. The scope of God's saving purpose is wonderfully broad—the everlasting covenant is established between God and "every living creature of all flesh" (v. 15)! Salvation is won for all—sinners, Pharisees, disciples, Gentiles—because the One who suffers death on the cross is none other than the Son of the God who created all things.

GETTING CLOSE TO GOD

Christ . . . suffered . . . in order to bring you to God (1 Peter 3:18-22; v. 18).

There is always a part of us that does not want to get too close to God. This is the result of our human rebellion. But we were created to be close to God, to walk with God, to live in God's presence. The suffering of God's Son places us before God where we encounter eternal lovingkindness.

ABRAHAM'S FAITH: PART I

. . . those who share the faith of Abraham (Romans 4:13-25; v. 16).

It all depends on God's promise, apart from what is humanly possible. Abraham believed God when there was nothing to count on, nothing that could be grasped, except the promise. Faith does not see (Hebrews 11:1), or feel. We believe that God will not forsake us, even if our economic security does. We believe in the forgiveness of sins, even though we may feel more guilty than innocent. Abraham's faith is our faith, and the righteousness "reckoned to Abraham" is ours as well, by grace through faith.

ABRAHAM'S FAITH: PART II

. . . the words "it was reckoned to him," were written not for his sake alone, but for ours also (Romans 4:13-25; v. 23).

God does not treat people differently. If righteousness was given to Abraham "by faith," then that is how God will deal with us also. The focus of our faith is Jesus. It is not faith in our faith, which leads to pride and turns out not to be faith at all. The focus of our faith is Jesus "who was handed over to death . . . and was raised for our justification" (v. 25).

ABRAHAM'S FAITH: PART III

[Abraham's] faith "was reckoned to him as righteousness" (Romans 4:13-25; v. 22).

Faith is possible only in the face of the most improbable propositions. That Abraham and Sarah would have a child when they are already old and "as good as dead" was improbable. Abraham believed God and was counted righteous. That God

31

could forgive sins on account of the death of Jesus on the cross may seem unfair for Jesus and improbable for us. Nevertheless this is how God has decided to deal with sin. When we believe it, we are numbered among the righteous.

THE NEW WAY

Make me to know your ways, O LORD (Psalm 25; v. 4).
We are all pretty much "set in our ways." To ask the Lord to show us his ways is a bit daring. What if God's way is to lead us away from deeply ingrained attitudes and ways of relating to other people? In Christ, there is a new creation (2 Corinthians 5:17). By faith in Christ we can expect that God will be continually renewing us, showing us the New Way. Before we ask to know the ways of the Lord, we probably need to pray for courage to know the ways of the Lord.

SUFFERING AND DEATH

. . . the Son of Man must undergo great suffering. . . . He said all this quite openly (Mark 8:31-38; v. 31).
Sin, evil, cross, death—these things are not pleasant to talk about. However, there is absolutely no reason to hide the cross from view or from our conversation. We would rather talk about victory and glory, but the salvation of the world depends on the suffering and death of Jesus Christ. The cross was made necessary by the presence of sin and evil in the world. We talk "quite openly" about the suffering and death of Jesus because that is how God wishes to deliver the world from sin and evil.

AFFLICTION

For he did not despise or abhor the affliction of the afflicted (Psalm 22:22-30; v. 24).
Gruesome injuries cause us to avert our gaze. It is easy to ignore the hardship of others; we wish other people would "just get over" their emotional pain. God, on the other hand, is compassionate. There is no hurt or pain or suffering that God does not see and feel. The cross of Jesus convinces us that even in suffering, abandonment and death, God is with us.

LENT
GOD'S PLAN
. . . divine things . . . human things . . . (Mark 8:31-38; v. 33).
Someone wrote that God's plan runs so counter to human expectations that it gives the appearance of no plan at all. Dying to live is the chief example. When we are weak, there is only God, and then we are suddenly strong. When we feel we have few resources, the Lord provides. In the market place it is the strongest and cleverest who survive. In the economy of the gospel it is sacrifice to benefit one's neighbor that leads to life. In one realm it is merit, in the other everything is by grace.

SELF-DENIAL
. . . deny themselves . . . (Mark 8:31-38; v. 34).
Suddenly it is hard to be a Christian! Self-denial runs exactly counter to our needs for self-affirmation and self-preservation. It is really about trust. Self-denial is throwing everything to the wind and trusting God. So there is generosity in almsgiving; there is service to neighbor, especially if it is costly to us; there is availability when we would rather have the time to ourselves. It is even giving up claims to righteousness, trusting that God will give this too by grace. Dying in order to live is the great open secret of the gospel life.

THE CROSS: PART I--FOOLISHNESS
The cross is foolishness to those who are perishing (1 Corinthians 1:18-25; v. 18).
The gospel seems to contradict the laws of nature at every turn. A drowning swimmer instinctively thrashes about, fighting against the lifeguard who comes to save. We naturally think we need to "do" something, "try harder," in order to be declared righteous. It is Christ who has done everything for us, on the cross. If we think we need to "do" something, we fight against the One who comes to save.

THE CROSS: PART II--POWER
The cross . . . is the power of God (1 Corinthians 1:18-25; v. 18).
Looking at it from another angle, the gospel still seems to contradict the laws of nature. The power of God is hidden in the

33

apparent weakness of the cross. It is just exactly in the cross of
Christ that the battle with sin and death and devil is won. That
victory is ours through our baptism into Christ's death.

THE CROSS: PART III-STUMBLING BLOCK
... Christ crucified ... a stumbling block ... (1 Corinthians 1:18-
25; v. 23).
It is reasonable to ask that things make sense. So when we lift high
the cross we suddenly find ourselves on the wrong side of
reasonableness. God's ways contradict conventional wisdom at
every turn. To a world searching for reasonableness God shows us
the crucified Messiah. His death is our life. His weakness is God's
power to free us from sin, death and evil.

OUR FATHER'S HOUSE
"Take these things out of here" (John 2:13-22; v. 16).
God's house is not a marketplace. God's house is nothing else,
either, except a place of prayer, praise and thanksgiving. It is where
the body of Christ becomes visible in sacramental form as well as
in the Assembled Body of Believers. For this reason there are
things that do not belong in God's house. Animosity, jealousy,
dissensions do not belong. Nor do features of human life that
divide—political association, nationality, or any other manner of
categorizing people for whatever purpose. In our Father's house
we acknowledge only one Lord, Jesus Christ.

THE NEW DEAL
"Stop making my Father's house a marketplace" (John 2:13-22;
v. 16).
God is not in the business of making deals, favoring some and
punishing others on the basis of our best bargains. Prosperity or
good fortune is not the result of perfect attendance at church or
clean living. On the other hand, neither is illness or adversity the
result of the sins of our youth. God's "deal" for us is forgiveness,
life and salvation through Jesus Christ. God meets us in the new
Temple, Jesus Christ, where we meet a God who gives us all things
by grace.

LENT
MEETING GOD
He was speaking of the temple of his body (John 2:13-22; v. 21).
The temple is where we meet God and where God meets us. In the temple there is painful acknowledgement that our efforts have fallen short, and things need to be made right. Jesus himself is the temple where God comes to us, and where we come to God. In the body of Jesus, through his pain and death, God makes things right.

"For some reason, I'm better when I'm in church. I don't know why." –an Illinois politician who stops to pray in churches along the campaign trail

---

FULFILLING THE LAW
The law of the LORD is perfect (Psalm 19; v. 7).
Monuments to the Ten Commandments on the courthouse lawn notwithstanding, perfection is a bit beyond our reach. It's one thing to show lawbreakers God's law chiseled in stone; it's another to hold God's commands up to one's face as to a mirror. We hang plaques on the walls of our homes with inspirational messages. Not many homes are decorated with the Ten Commandments. This is because the law is perfect, and we are not. We place our faith in Christ, who is the fulfillment of the law for us.

RESURRECTION: PART I
You were dead (Ephesians 2:1-10; v. 1).
While we wait for the Great Resurrection let us not fail to notice the resurrections that take place around us every day. By God's grace in Jesus Christ, people overcome addiction; they give up bad attitudes; they make amends with someone they have wronged; they become aware of the presence of Jesus Christ in their lives. Maybe a resurrection will occur in your life today.

RESURRECTION: PART II
. . . we were dead . . . [God] made us alive . . . (Ephesians 2:1-10; v. 5).
The more radically we can state this the more exciting our faith becomes. To acknowledge our previous condition as death is simply to turn everything over to God and then wait and see. What

35

is God up to in our lives? Then, in the power of God's Spirit we are raised with Christ from death to life, from sin to righteousness, from despair to joy. The more we resist the idea of our previous death the more we miss out on the wonder of God's grace for us.

RESURRECTION: PART III

. . . we are what he has made us (Ephesians 2:1-10; v. 10).

"Just as I am, I come," surely, but now we are not what we used to be. There has been a resurrection, a mini-resurrection, in no way comparable with the Great Resurrection on the day of the Lord, but a change, a transformation. We are new persons, raised in the image of Christ. Dead to sin and alive to God. Not scurrying off into another room but seeking God's company day to day and hour to hour. Living in the light of Christ, fleeing from the darkness of the past. Day by day, when we remember to whom we belong, we will notice how God is transforming our lives.

RESURRECTION: PART IV

By grace you have been saved through faith . . . it is the gift of God (Ephesians 2:1-10; v. 8).

That light flooding your soul and filling you with an indescribable sense of well-being, contentment and love for everyone and everything around you is God's grace, revealed in Jesus Christ. It is gift. We didn't invent it, or deserve it, or even expect it. It is in this grace that our faith is located, and it is to this grace that we bear witness.

PERILOUS WILDERNESS

Some wandered in desert wastes (Psalm 107:1-15; v. 4).

Moving from slavery to the Promised Land means crossing the desert. The chief peril of the desert is not the heat or the lack of food and water. The chief temptation of the desert is to look longingly to our past. Whatever it is that God has freed us from needs to be left behind. The wilderness is only perilous if we forget that God is leading us.

GOD SO LOVED THE WORLD

For God so loved the world that he gave his only Son, so that everyone who believes in him may not perish but may have eternal life (John 3:14-21; v. 16).

The child in Sunday school did not believe that he could memorize a Bible verse three lines long! But he read through the verse and *voilá!* It was already fixed in his mind. The universal appeal of this verse is revealed in the first line: God so loved "the world." The arms of God stretched out on the cross of Christ to embrace the world proclaim the irresistible love of God for all people, languages, tribes and nations.

LOST AND FOUND

Those who believe in him are not condemned (John 3:14-21; v. 18). Here is good news for those who have lost their way in the wilderness due to their mistakes or foolishness. Turn to Jesus, believe in him, and there is no condemnation. However fierce and inhospitable the world may be, those who fix their eyes on Jesus have nothing to fear, least of all condemnation.

INTERESTED GREEKS

Some Greeks . . . said, "Sir, we wish to see Jesus" (John 12:20-26; v. 21).

We should not assume that the "Greeks" are not interested in the Christian faith. Those outside the Christian community may not be interested in church, nor even in associating with Christians, but the person of Jesus Christ has always and will continue to fascinate and attract the whole human community. It is Jesus they wish to know, not "church," not "programs to fit every need." When they come asking to see Jesus, what will we say?

A USEFUL SEED

"Unless a grain of wheat falls into the earth and dies, it remains just a single grain; but if it dies, it bears much fruit (John 12:20-26; v. 24).

The call to discipleship—denial of self in order to find life—finds its truth in this example from nature. A wheat seed only becomes useful by giving up its life, either to be planted or ground up for flour and consumed. Jesus leads the way to show the truth of this saying. Looking at the cross, who could have imagined the resurrection? Just as the seed gives no hint of the fruit, so we cannot imagine what self-denial will look like on the other side of our cross.

THE GLORY OF THE FATHER
"Father, glorify your name" (John 12:27-33; v. 28).
The glory of God the Father is the Son who gave His Life for the life of the world. We give glory and honor to the Name of God when we turn in faith to the Son who redeems us from sin, death and the power of evil. We glorify God the Father when the Spirit instructs us and leads us and helps us to grow into the New Life that the Son has given us.

THE LIFTING UP
"I, when I am lifted up from the earth, will draw all people to myself" (John 12:27-33).
Of all the wonders of the world, ancient and modern, none surpasses the "lifting up" of Jesus Christ, his exaltation on the cross. God is in the flesh, not expressing pity for the human race from a distance, but here, in human agony, in love poured out for you and for me and for everyone who knows what it is to be human. In the end it is not the wisdom of Jesus, nor even his miracles, that attract. It is the cross that draws all people to this most wondrous love.

What sins have you committed since we last met?
--John Wesley (1703-1791)

TRUTH
You desire truth in the inward being (Psalm 51:1-12; v. 6).
We know all the tricks to account for our mistakes. We rationalize and make excuses, we blame someone else. By nature we do everything except admit our mistake. God desires a ruthlessly truthful heart. In the presence of God we can dare to be honest. An

honest, forthright confession results in forgiveness that is full, complete, and absolutely trustworthy, for Jesus' sake.

JOY

Restore to me the joy of your salvation (Psalm 51:1-12; v. 12).

The glow and inner joy seen in people new to faith in Christ may amaze or even irritate those of us who can never remember a time when we were not Christians. Perhaps we are even envious and wonder how we could get some of that. We cannot create our own joy, and even when commanded ("Rejoice always" e.g.) it is only to reawaken what God has already placed in our hearts. Joy is always a gift, a fruit of the Spirit (Galatians 5:22). When we sit back, open our hands and heart, our soul and mind, and let the grace of the Lord Jesus fill us, behold! A joy that can only come from God.

SPONTANEOUS LOVE

I will put my law within them (Jeremiah 31:31-34; v. 33).

The difference between doing something under compulsion and doing the same thing with joy and gladness in your heart is quality. We do a thing better if we are happy about doing it in the first place. As long as the law of God is imposed on us obedience to it will be a problem. In Christ, the will of God is implanted in our hearts. Love for God and love for neighbor come spontaneously, from within, when we are in Christ, and Christ is in us.

A HOLY PLACE

Jesus entered once for all into the Holy Place . . . with his own blood (Hebrews 9:11-15; v. 12).

There is a Holy Place where God would meet us if only we had the courage to enter. We do not know how to take care of ourselves and we have messed up the world in which we live. It is sin that separates us from God and sin that cries out for redemption. Jesus entered the Holy Place shedding blood on our behalf. It is Jesus Christ himself who has become that Holy Place and who opens the door, and invites us in to be in God's presence.

WITH UTMOST REVERENCE

. . . at the name of Jesus every knee should bend . . . (Philippians 2:5-11; v. 10).

It is all too easy to say the Name, the holy Name of Jesus, who is Lord of us. This ancient hymn quoted in Philippians suggests the solemn gesture of bending the knee at every utterance of the Sacred Name. The Name of Jesus is guarded with utmost reverence because of his obedience to the Father's will. By his death and resurrection, Jesus has brought forgiveness of sins, life and salvation into our troubled world. Glory, honor, and exaltation to the Name above every name!

THE ORIGIN OF FAITH

But I trust in you, O LORD; I say, "You are my God" (Psalm 31; v. 14).

Faith has its origin in emptiness, adversity, and despair. When we are full, when things are going well, we may remember to give thanks to God. But faith begins to emerge when distress, scorn grief and sighing come upon us. When we have nothing, we throw ourselves on God, and we find out what faith is all about. It is the faith of Jesus who, even in the abandonment of the cross, was able to cry out, "My God!"

MAUNDY THURSDAY

"Love for one another" (John 13:1-17, 31b-35; v. 35).

"Other worldly" thoughts evaporate pretty quickly in the light of the "new commandment" which Jesus gave his disciples on the night of his betrayal—to love one another. If we are looking heavenward to find God, or inward to find ourselves, Jesus redirects our gaze to find our brothers and sisters right here, beside us. The commandment is not to "like" people, but to love them. The different between 'like' and 'love' is sacrifice.

LOOKING FOR JESUS
"Whom are you looking for?" . . . "I am he" (John 18:1-11; vv. 4, 5).
Judas, soldiers, priestly police and Pharisees as well! With vastly different needs and purposes they were looking for Jesus. We come looking for Jesus, perhaps knowing only that our need for Jesus is as deep as life itself. "I am he." The God revealed to Moses at Sinai is the God revealed in Jesus Christ, the One we have been looking for, the One who saw us "under the fig tree" (John 1:48) even before we were looking for Jesus.

WHERE GOD MEETS US
"My God, my God, why? (Mark 15:33-39; v. 34).
The most sincere prayer ever prayed by the Most Righteous One who ever lived is answered with silence. All our attempts to ponder the mechanics of the cross end in the same question, Why? We may have been asking the wrong question. It is not Why, but Who? The centurion tells us: "Truly, this man was God's Son" (v. 39). We are drawn to God in love and faith by the cross of Christ, and that is where God's love meets us.

GOOD FRIDAY
"It is finished" (John 19:30).
On this solemn day, so heavy with the thought that the Son of God has been humbled by scorn, rejected, and undergone the worst sort of suffering devised by evil minds, it is a wonder that the sun even bothers to rise, or that routine affairs of home and industry can be conducted. Life goes on just exactly because "It is finished." God's work of redeeming this world from sin, death and devil was accomplished on that Friday so many years ago. It is our faith in this word, "It is finished," that gives the sun and moon courage to watch over this world, and for life to go on.

III. Easter

If Christ is risen, nothing else matters;
And if Christ is not risen, nothing else matters.
--Jaroslav Pelikan (1923-2006)

TERROR AND AMAZEMENT
They fled from the tomb, for terror and amazement had seized them
(Mark 16:1-8; v. 8).
Mark's narration of the resurrection seems to end abruptly. "A
young man" (an angel?) told the women, "Do not be alarmed."
Nevertheless, they ran away, for "terror and amazement had seized
them." Of course they fled! Whoever heard of someone rising from
the dead?! Let the news of Christ's rising from the tomb send a
tremor up and down your spine of amazement, excitement,
admiration, and joy.

WHAT ABOUT THE STONE?
Who will roll away the stone for us? (Mark 16:1-8; v. 3).
The women were up early, bought what they needed, but on the
way they remembered one more thing: "What about the stone?" If
we do too much planning we may miss out on the Big Event. The
women did not let the heavy stone deter them. They proceeded to
the tomb and found that God had already resolved the issue, and in
a way they could not have imagined. In God's kingdom, obstacles
are no obstacles.

THE CENTRAL POINT
Jesus of Nazareth . . . has been raised (Mark 16:1-8; v. 6).
Amid all of the other interesting details of Easter, the central point
cannot be lost on us. Jesus of Nazareth has been raised from the
dead. The Jesus who talked of loving one's enemies, who healed
the sick and ate with sinners, who was crucified, died and was
buried, has been raised. Jesus is alive! And so is the power of his

message and mission. "Jesus has been raised" is God's word which answers our fears and doubts, our questions and hesitations.

CALLED BY NAME

Mary Magdalene went and announced to the disciples, "I have seen the Lord" (John 20:1-18; v. 18).

Mary Magdalene is one of the heroic, unsung people of the Bible. Standing close to his cross on Good Friday, now coming to the tomb early, what did she expect to do or see? Even when it seemed the mission and purpose of Jesus had been crushed, she was there. Then, in a remarkable twist, as she was immersed in her sorrow and perplexity, Jesus comes to her and calls her by name. Mary Magdalene, apostle to the apostles, is the first to announce the good news of the resurrection. Do you hear Jesus calling your name?

THIS IS THE DAY!

. . . glad songs of victory in the tents of the righteous . . . (Psalm 118; v. 15).

This is the day the Lord has made. It is resurrection from death to life. It is the oppression of sin and evil one day, and then, in the power of God, it is triumph, victory, life, joy and gladness the next. Sin is defeated. Death is conquered. All the petty lords and masters who thought they could give us life have been set aside. We have a new Master, Jesus, the Lord of us, who reigns with forgiveness, compassion and love. He enables us also to imitate him and serve him in his kingdom of peace and joy.

HOLDING FIRMLY

. . . if you hold firmly to the message (1 Corinthians 15:1-11; v. 2).

The daily ritual of remembering one's baptism enables us to hold firmly to the message. When we remember our baptism we remember that "Christ is risen! Alleluia! Risen indeed! Alleluia!" And we, too, with Christ, have been raised to a new life. The old Adam/Eve in us will allow the newness of Easter to fade away into the way things used to be. Holding firmly to the message that Christ is risen! and we with him, the wonder and amazement of Easter become brighter and brighter day by day.

44

A FEARFUL TESTIMONY

. . . so you have come to believe (1 Corinthians 15:1-11; v. 11).
If they had found a corpse there would be nothing to be afraid of.
But they found an empty tomb and a messenger. There have been
many messengers, some with articulate testimonies, some merely
with incoherent utterances that Something Really Different has
taken place. By their word and in the power of the Holy Spirit, we
have come to believe. Now that we have heard the news, we also
are witnesses.

NOTHING ELSE MATTERS

"Peace be with you" (John 20:19-23; v. 19).
Even with imagination it is hard for us, with two thousand years of
Tradition behind us, to put ourselves in the locked room with the
disciples. Their trauma was unique, but not unrelated to the
traumas that affect us deeply. Whether it is profound loss or trivial
anxiety, the message of the risen Lord Jesus is the same. "Peace be
with you!" Jesus lives, and nothing else matters.

SENT

"Peace be with you . . . so I send you" (John 20:19-23; v. 21).
The Father sent Jesus to reveal God's love to the world. Jesus did
this in his words and deeds, and most especially on the cross. "So
I send you." In the peace of Jesus Christ, we are sent to speak to
our neighbors in Jesus' name, to let our deeds embody the love of
God, and especially, to take up the cross. It is the self-offering of
Christian people that will make Christ known. The "sending"
causes us to swallow hard, but we are always sent in the peace of
the risen Lord Jesus Christ.

OIL ON THE BEARD

*How very good and pleasant it is when kindred live together in
unity* (Psalm 133; v. 1).
The allusion to "oil running down the beard of Aaron" is not
meaningful to us, but when kindred live together in unity it is
indeed "very good and pleasant." It is possible because of

45

forgiveness of sin in Jesus' name. The secret of living together in close quarters is daily and mutual forgiveness of sins.

Faith
is either a struggle,
or it is nothing.
                                        –Helmut Thielicke (1908-1986)

THOMAS: PART I
"Unless I see . . . I will not believe" (John 20:24-31; v. 25).
We should not be too hard on doubting Thomas. Hebrews 11:1 ("Faith is . . . the conviction of things not seen") had not been written yet. Moreover, Thomas is merely saying what we all say from time to time. Faith is hard work, but faith is essentially "not seeing." It must have been frustrating for the other disciples when Thomas doubted their testimony. It is daunting for us as well, on the cusp as we are of becoming a witnessing people. What if they will not listen? We will do as the disciples did. They gave witness and left it up to God.

THOMAS: PART II
"Blessed are those who have not seen and yet have come to believe" (John 20:24-31; v. 29).
Jesus is talking to Thomas but he has not forgotten about us. We do not see the risen Lord much less his wounds. The signs we have are bread and wine gathered up in the word. Even with the risen Lord standing in front of him, faith was not easy for Thomas. It is neither easier nor harder for us. Faith is the gift of the Holy Spirit, and believing, Jesus calls us "blessed."

THE ORIGIN OF JOY
. . . in their joy . . . disbelieving ... wondering (Luke 24:36-43; v. 41).
Joy cannot be manufactured or faked. The joy the disciples felt originated when they caught sight of the risen Lord standing in their midst. Our joy originates in the Holy Spirit who allows us to see the crucified and risen body of Christ in bread and wine; and

who convinces us that we were buried and raised with Christ to newness of life; and whose Power envelopes us in prayer and worship. This joy bounces back and forth between disbelieving and wondering. We walk by faith, to be sure, but our Unknown Companion is Jesus Christ.

A GENEROUS EXPERIMENT

There was not a needy person among them (Acts 4:32-35; v. 34). Against this brief glimpse of the reality of the kingdom of God we throw up a thousand reasons why this experiment did not last long. Here is the testimony of the first believers: let it be known now and for all time that, in the power of the resurrection, when Christians gave it all up there was not a needy person among them. The brighter Easter glows in our hearts, the more generous and unselfish we become.

WIPED OUT

Repent . . . so that you sins may be wiped out (Acts 3:12-19; v. 19). Some modern day church leaders are reluctant to talk about repentance because it is a "downer." The joy of Easter's promise of resurrection is experienced by people who know they are going to die. The joy of Easter's victory over sin and evil is experienced by people who know they are sinners. The call to repentance is always heard in the context of forgiveness. Why should we repent? So that our sin may be wiped out! Thanks be to God for his suffering Messiah!

NEW GLASSES

He opened their minds to understand the scriptures (Luke 24:36b-48; v. 45). New glasses helped the disciples to see and understand the scriptures in a different way. They saw Jesus in Scripture, and Jesus as the fulfillment of Scripture. The Bible is the manger, Martin Luther said, that holds Christ. We will see with new eyes if, as we open the book to read, we look for Christ on every page.

DISTURBED BY MANY THINGS
When you are disturbed, do not sin (Psalm 4; v. 4).
When we feel that others are taking advantage of us, it is a great Temptation to respond in kind. If they shout, we shout back. If they go behind our back, we lie awake planning how we can do the same to them. We will be disturbed by many things in life. The psalmist advises us to be careful of letting a disturbed spirit draw us into sin. Better to "be silent," and "put your trust in the Lord." Then we "sleep in peace," and we awake to find that God has "put gladness in our heart."

COPYRIGHT
The Author of life (Acts 3:12-19; v. 15).
Jesus has the copyright on life. That is the bold assertion of his Apostle Peter, who calls Jesus the author, the originator, of life. There are other philosophies and ideas that people can organize their lives around but we believe, without arrogance or judgment, that life as God the Creator meant it to be is attained through faith in Jesus Christ.

DRAWN TO THE CENTER
See what love the Father has given us, that we should be called children of God (1 John 3:1-7; v. 1).
God does not want to be at the edge of our lives, but at the center. The whole purpose of the Incarnation of Jesus was to show God's love for us and to draw us to the center, where God is. Those who have not experienced reconciliation with our heavenly Father put God out at the edge, in fear. God's Spirit brings us to faith in Christ, who gathers us into God's warm embrace.

THE GOOD SHEPHERD: PART I
"I am the good shepherd" (John 10:11-18; v. 11).
The "I AM" sayings of Jesus recall the name of God revealed to Moses at the burning bush. "Tell them I AM has sent me to you" (Exodus 3:14). We are to understand that the God who delivered Israel from slavery has become flesh and blood in Jesus, and the

One who leads us will rescue us from every bad thing, because he is the "good" shepherd.

THE GOOD SHEPHERD: PART II

"I am the good shepherd. I know my own" (John 10:11-18; v. 14). Before we can claim to know Jesus, Jesus already has claimed us, known us, and made us his own people. Our knowledge of Jesus is always imperfect, inadequate, and partial. It doesn't matter. Our faith is kindled by this word, that Jesus knows us. It is in clinging to this promise that we grow in our knowledge of the Lord Jesus Christ.

THE GOOD SHEPHERD: PART III

"My own know me" (John 10:11-18; v. 14).
Which Jesus do you know? The one who says, "Come to me and I will give you rest" or the one who says, "Take up your cross and follow me"? The answer is Yes—Jesus gives both rest and challenge. "I want to know Christ and the power of his resurrection and the sharing of his sufferings" (Philippians 3:10).

THE GOOD SHEPHERD: PART IV

". . . there will be one flock, one shepherd" (John 10:11-18; v. 16). It did not take long for the church to splinter into factions. "I belong to Paul," some said. "I belong to Apollos," said others (1 Corinthians 1:12). Today just about anyone with the first month's rent can open a store front to start a "church," and be a "bishop" to boot. Sadly, Christ's church has a hard time speaking with one voice. There are doctrinal, moral and ethical opinions to satisfy any desire. As long as Jesus is willing to allow sinners into his Church divisions are bound to occur. In the end, happily, "There will be one flock, one shepherd." It is the promise of the God Shepherd.

THE GOOD SHEPHERD: PART V

I shall not want (Psalm 23; v. 1).
"I want . . . this or that" is one of the first things we learn to say, and one of the hardest things to give up. Even our prayers are filled with incessant "wanting" of this or that. The Good Shepherd will

care for us in every need. It is the Spirit's gift to lead us to the place where we have absolute trust in the "goodness and mercy" of the Lord and we can finally say, "I shall not want."

CHRIST-LIKE
. . . we will be like him, for we will see him as he is (1 John 3:1-7; v. 2).

Our goal from day to day, as we face life, and the challenges the world brings our way, is to be "Christ-like." Now we see Christ by faith through the witness of Scripture, especially the witness of his death and resurrection. When sight replaces faith, we will be like him in love, in holiness, in perfect communion with God and with God's people.

YHWH
. . . by the name of Jesus Christ of Nazareth . . . (Acts 4:5-12; v. 10).

If God revealed his name to Moses by those Four Sacred Letters, YHWH, now God has shown his face, will, purpose, and love in JESUS CHRIST. In the Name of JESUS there is healing, forgiveness of sins, and power to move into the New Creation. In the Name of JESUS broken relationships are mended and life in community hints at the perfect life to come. "Whatever you do, in word or deed, do in the name of the Lord Jesus" (Colossians 3:17).

SURRENDERING OUR WEAPONS
. . . no other name . . . (Acts 4:5-12; v. 12).

If our proclamation of Jesus as the only Name comes across as arrogant or exclusive, the problem may be that we have proclaimed ourselves rather than Christ. Jesus was the obedient servant, humble even to death on the cross. There is no arrogance in Jesus. "No other name" is not a weapon to use against other religious faiths, but a gracious invitation into fellowship with God through Jesus Christ, bringing the possibility that all weapons, especially religious weapons, may be surrendered, so that Jesus, and not one's religion, is the basis for human community.

Easter

THE VINE: PART I

"I am the vine, you are the branches. Those who abide in me and I in them bear much fruit" (John 15:1-8; v. 5).

Cut off from Christ the Vine, we would be powerless to love either neighbor or God, ineffective against temptation, and hopeless when the shadows lengthen. But we are in Christ, and he feeds us through Word and Sacrament and prayer, filling our hearts with his Spirit, putting love in our hearts, giving us a cheerful countenance in every opportunity to serve.

THE VINE: PART II

"He removes every branch that bears no fruit" (John 15:1-8; v. 2).

Good gardeners have no pity. When a plant does not do well, they pluck it up and give its space to another. It sounds incredibly harsh to think that our heavenly Father removes branches from Christ the Vine. Focused as we are almost exclusively on grace, our hearts are not inclined toward a God who judges. God's judgment, however, is whether we allow the grace of the Lord Jesus to flow into our hearts to produce the fruits of faith, hope, and love.

THE VINE: PART III

"If you abide in me . . . ask . . ." (John 15:1-8; v. 7).

"Ask and it will be done." The promise seems too great, too broad, too wonderful. In proportion to our faith, maybe it is. It depends on the "abide in me." Those who abide in Christ are attuned to his will, and through Christ to the will of the Father. In Christ we ask that he may be revealed in us and through us. In Christ we ask that the power and glory of his death and resurrection may be effective in our world. Ask, and it will be done for you.

DIVINE SERVICE

From you comes my praise in the great congregation . . . (Psalm 22:25-31; v. 25).

This prayer begins on Good Friday ("My God, my God, why?") and brings us to Easter (". . . my praise"). We come into God's presence with nothing except a profound sense of abandonment. Then, by God's grace and power, we are aware of outside help.

51

"*From you* comes my praise." The old term for worship was "Divine Service," which means God serves us through word, font and table. Even our praise is God's gift to us!

A QUESTION
. . . all who sleep in the earth [shall] bow down (Psalm 22:25-31; v. 29).
At the end, the Question: Now what? God's promise is that "all who sleep in the earth" will by no means be left out of the honor and privilege of acknowledging Jesus Christ as Lord. "All who sleep in the earth" will "live for him" and find that in Jesus Christ, the Forsaken One (22:1), no one is finally forsaken. All, even those who sleep in the dust, will find that Jesus Christ means life, joy, glory and honor forever.

LEFT BEHIND
This is a wilderness road . . . Look, here is water (Acts 8:26-40; vv. 26, 36).
"Some wandered in desert wastes" (Psalm 107:4), searching for meaning and truth and a purpose for life. All of a sudden, there is water. There is a washing and renewal. Old Adam/Eve are left behind with Pharaoh's chariots and we go on our way rejoicing in the company of Christ our Lord, who makes "the wilderness a pool of water, and the dry land springs of water" (Isaiah 41:18).

SEALED BY THE SPIRIT
By this we know that we abide in him and he in us, because he has given us of his Spirit (1 John 4:7-21; v. 13).
It is a great comfort to know for sure that Christ "abides in us" and we in him. The sign that lets us know that this is true is the presence of the Spirit. Since we do not always "feel" the Spirit, the question lingers. Let us be confident that we abide in Christ and he in us because at baptism we were "sealed by the Spirit and marked with the cross of Christ forever."

ASCENSION DAY: PART I
". . . until you have been clothed with power from on high" Luke 24:44-53; v. 49).

The risen Lord who surprised the disciples with his appearing after his death and burial now surprises again with his disappearance. He is taken away into glory and honor forever, yet we are not alone. The glorious Lord of all, Jesus Christ, clothes us with his Holy Spirit, the power from on high. "I am with you always," to comfort in sadness and empower for service.

ASCENSION DAY: PART II
"You will be my witnesses" (Acts 1:1-11; v. 8).

We are not ambassadors for a religious institution or heralds of our good works. We are witness of Jesus Christ, not of ourselves. God has prepared 'good works' for us to do (Ephesians 2:10), but our works do not comprise our witness. What if we manage to find ways to serve our neighbor, or if we manage some level of love for the unlovable? Maybe even non-believers will do this and do it better. We are not promoting ourselves. We are witnesses of Jesus Christ, his death and resurrection, his love for all people, his gift of forgiveness and new life. Our message is Christ.

My teacher is Jesus Christ;
my food is Jesus Christ;
the source of my actions is Jesus Christ.

–Coptic monk

THE JOY OF JESUS
"I have said these things to you so that my joy may be in you" (John 15:9-17; v. 11).

We were made for companionship and fellowship with God. "Our hearts are restless till they find their rest in you," prayed St. Augustine. Jesus Christ, our friend, brings us into the presence of God where God gazes on us with love and admiration, taking pleasure in what he has created. To be at home with God, knowing that we *belong* there, is to share the joy of Jesus.

FRIENDS

"I have called you friends, because I have made known to you everything that I have heard from my Father" (John 15:12-17; v. 15).

Between friends there is a transparency that keeps nothing back, nothing hidden. With Jesus there are no secret teachings, no deep mysteries that only the spiritual giants can discover. With Jesus everything is disclosed. In Jesus we know that the will of God for us is to be loved with the sacrificial love of Christ, and that we, his friends, should offer ourselves to each other and to our neighbor in the same way.

CHOSEN

"You did not choose me but I chose you. And I appointed you to . . . bear fruit" (John 15:12-17; v. 16).

What a thrill it is to be chosen! Let no day go by without feeling that surge of ecstasy that comes from hearing Jesus call your name. We are chosen, and appointed . . . to bear fruit. On this day we have been chosen by Jesus to bring "love, joy, peace, patience, kindness, generosity . . ." (Galatians 5:22) to some person or some situation that we will encounter. What a thrill it is to know that Jesus is counting on us!

VICTORY

. . . the victory that conquers the world is our faith (1 John 5:1-6; v. 4).

We thought we had pretty much made friends with the world, until we noticed that the world is for revenge; we announce forgiveness. The world is content to have enemies and name them; we love our enemies and pray for those who give us a hard time. The world is willing to let people put their own interests first; Christians look to the needs of others before their own. The worldly forces are arrayed against us. What changes us and changes the world is our faith in the Lord Jesus Christ.

GRACE FILLED WITNESS

God gave us eternal life, and this life is in his Son (1 John 5:9-13; v. 11).

Here is where we can see the difference between a grace filled witness and a witness based on fear. Some believers in Jesus climb up on the judge's bench and enter a judgment against those who do not believe. This sort of witness appeals to fear rather than love. In our witness the emphasis is on the gift. God's gift is eternal life in Jesus. This is what we believe and proclaim.

GOD'S ANSWER

I write these things . . . so that you may know that you have eternal life (1 John 5:9-13; v. 13).

It is our instinct to cling to this life for all we're worth, and for good reason. This life is God's gift to all of us, and in this life God wants us to enjoy every blessing. This life counts, and how we live this life matters. If, as the sands of our life run out, we are troubled by the brevity and precarious nature of this life, it troubles God as well. God's answer is the resurrection of Jesus, and the promise of our own resurrection to eternal life is a measure of God's grace.

BELONGING: PART I

"They were yours, and you gave them to me . . . all mine are yours, and yours are mine" (John 16:6-19; vv. 6, 10).

A great transaction has taken place in Christ. We are God's people, and for that reason God the Father entrusted us to Christ's care. For us the Good Shepherd gave his life and saved us from sin death, and devil. We belong to Christ, and for that very reason we belong to God.

BELONGING: PART II

"They do not belong to the world, just as I do not belong to the world" (John 17:6-19; v. 14).

With our attachments to place or country, to institution or ideology, perhaps we are shocked to learn that we do not belong to this world. We *belong* to God through Jesus Christ. Jesus did not belong to this world with its idolatries, false values and empty pursuits. However, it was just exactly in "not belonging" that enabled Jesus to love the world. In the same way, just as through Christ we belong to God, we, as disciples of Jesus, are free to love the world in the same sacrificial way.

HEARING THE WORD
. . . the Holy Spirit fell upon all who heard the word (Acts 10:44-48; v. 44).

Whenever the word of Jesus is proclaimed, the Holy Spirit is there to bring about the obedience of faith, and to fill the believer's heart with the joy of Jesus. It is no less true today than on that day in the house of Cornelius. As we listen to the good news of Jesus Christ, we might just discover the power of God's Spirit at work in our midst as well.

THE RIGHTEOUS FLOURISH
They are like trees planted by streams of water (Psalm 1; v. 3).

Jesus says of those whom God gave to his care, "They have kept your word" (John 17:6). God's word is where the righteous draw water and flourish. Anxieties burn and wither our spirits like the sun and wind, but God's word is the stream of water that keeps our leaves green and our fruit sweet. Those who are fed by God's word keep on producing the fruits of peace, love, joy and patience. If we find we are drying up, we know where to turn to find water.

UNANSWERED PRAYER
Teacher, do you not care? (Mark 4:35-41; v. 38).

This is the cry of everyone who struggles with unanswered prayer. The problem is not that God does not see or does not care, but that our thoughts are not God's thoughts, nor our ways God's ways (Isaiah 55). We cry to the Lord from the depths just exactly because we know that God does care.

THE THING TO FEAR

"Why are you afraid? Have you still no faith?" (Mark 4:35-41; v. 40).

The disciples were counting on Jesus, but one gets the impression that Jesus was counting on the faith of the disciples to pull them through the storm. If Jesus chides his disciples for lack of faith, it means that Jesus *expects* his disciples to be full of solid, absolute trust in God in all circumstances. In the middle of the storm, the thing to fear is not the strong wind but weak faith.

God, most days I think the hardest thing I have to do is to pray.
--a Bishop

IN DYING, THEY LIVE: PART I

. . . as dying, and see, we are alive (2 Corinthians 6:1-13; v. 9).

We gape in astonishment at the witness of the Apostle Paul. Lesser souls would have given up at the hint of affliction or hardship. The only explanation that accounts for persistence through calamity and beating is the gospel of Jesus Christ. The Holy Spirit is able to convince righteous people and the wicked alike that what God has accomplished in Jesus Christ to defeat sin and death is all that matters. Those who take up the cross of Jesus discover, to their amazement, that even in dying they live!

IN DYING, THEY LIVE: PART II

. . . as dying, and see, we are alive (2 Corinthians 6:1-13; v. 9).

The Christian life is lived under a series of apparent contradictions. If you give up your life for the sake of the gospel, you will find it, Jesus taught. The power of God is revealed in the weakness of the cross. Beware of triumphalism in the Christian arena. The triumph comes after the resurrection. In the meantime, we bear the cross, and that is exactly where we find our Savior Jesus Christ.

NO PLACE FOR WHINERS

. . . as servants of God we have commended ourselves . . . through hardships . . . (2 Corinthians 6:1-13; v. 4).

Followers of Jesus cannot be whiners. It is the way of the cross for us. Perhaps we are really working hard, doing good works, striving for peace and justice, and no one cares! Or worse, they level criticisms against us and actually work against us. Never mind. Whatever hardships come our way, the cry is the same: "See, we are alive!" In the power of the resurrection the Lord Jesus is in command over every foe and danger. When clouds gather, his word to us is "Peace, be still!"

A DAY OF GRACE

Now is the day of salvation (2 Corinthians 6:1-13; v. 2).

After a while the dawns start to look alike. Or do they? The first light breaks the darkness and behold! God is giving us another day of grace, a day in which the resurrection of Jesus Christ overpowers the darkness of sin and evil. Grace, mercy and peace come flooding into our lives as God's answer to our anguish, stress or pain. Christ, who died, now is risen, and raises us also out of the shambles of yesterday into newness of life today. Today, now, this is the day of salvation!

SANCTIFY THEM: PART I

"The words that you gave to me I have given to them" (John 17:6-12; v. 8).

We must be careful how we draw the picture of our God, neither making God too small nor lapsing into mere speculation. The mystery of the fullness of God is not ours to know. What is ours to know is the God revealed to us through Jesus Christ. This much of God will occupy our thoughts and imagination and instill in us love and devotion for a lifetime. The words that Jesus has given to us reveal what we need to know about God's nature and purpose. Jesus has given us "the words of eternal life" (John 6:68).

SANCTIFY THEM: PART II

". . . that they may have my joy made complete in themselves" John
17:11-19; v. 13).

On the way to Gethsemane, trial and crucifixion, Jesus finds it in
his heart to say something about joy. The joy of Jesus is not
mindless giddiness, oblivious to the realities of discipleship. The
source of Jesus' joy is the Holy Father, who has given Jesus all
things and who will, in spite of the world's hatred, "protect them"
and "sanctify them." All things have been given to Christ, and we
belong to Christ. It is the source of our joy whatever else may
happen.

SANCTIFY THEM: PART III

*"They do not belong to the world, just as I do not belong to the
world"* (John 17:6-19; v. 14).

With our attachments to place or country, to institution or
ideology, perhaps we are shocked to learn that we do not belong to
this world. We *belong* to God through Jesus Christ. Jesus did not
belong to this world, with its idolatries, false values and empty
pursuits. However, it was "not belonging" that enabled Jesus to
"love the world" (John 3:16). In the same way, "just as," through
Christ we belong to God, we are free to love the world "Just as"
Jesus did.

SANCTIFY THEM: PART IV

"Sanctify them in the truth; your word is truth" (John 17:6-19; v.
17).

Jesus asks that the heavenly Father will make us holy, sanctified,
set apart for God's service and praise. People who are "holier than
thou" give sanctification a bad reputation. We do not make
ourselves over into the image of Christ. That is the work of the
Holy Spirit, sent by the Father, working through God's word.
God's word has the power to change and transform, bringing our
lives into conformity with our true nature, restored through Christ,
who is both Word and Truth.

Easter

IV. Pentecost

Come, Holy Ghost, our souls inspire
And lighten with celestial fire;
Thou the anointing Spirit art
Who dost thy sevenfold gifts impart.
Praise to thy eternal merit,
Father Son, and Holy Spirit

--Veni, creator Spiritus
Tr. John Cosin, 1594-1672

OUR GUIDE: PART I

"When the Spirit of truth comes he will guide you into all the truth" (John 16:12-15; v. 13).

We should not despair if we do not understand everything right now. No one understands everything all at once. The Spirit is our guide. If we are open to it, each day the Spirit will give us more and more insight into Christ, who is the Way, the Truth and the Life.

OUR GUIDE: PART II

"The Spirit . . . will guide you into all the truth" (John 16:12-15; v. 13).

When we think of the outpouring of the Holy Spirit perhaps what comes to mind is the frenzy of Pentecost, with tongues and such things. The Spirit has others gifts, however, which are just as important—lest frenzied, perhaps, but just as spectacular. The Spirit will guide us into all truth, to make us wise! The work of the Spirit is to lead us to Jesus, who is the truth. The Spirit guides us to truth and wisdom by anchoring our lives solidly in the death and resurrection of Jesus.

A BREATH OF FRESH AIR

When you send forth your spirit, they are created (Psalm 104:24-34; v. 30).

Breathing fresh air is a universal pleasure. The experience of gasping for air is likewise a universal horror. God's Spirit, God's Breath, sometimes blows, and, to our dismay, sometimes God's Breath is withheld. If we find ourselves suffocating in a mixture of anxiety, guilt, resentments, fears, or other bad attitudes we exhale a cry of despair and suddenly the Breath of God is there to fill heart and mind and soul with the life-giving grace of the Lord Jesus.

A GOOD LAWYER

". . . the Advocate . . . will testify on my behalf" (John 15:26-27; v. 26).

Even Jesus needs a good lawyer! In some languages the word for lawyer is "advocate." Just as the Spirit interprets and gives expression to our prayers, so, too, the Spirit, the Advocate, is present whenever the name of Jesus is mentioned. Even in our trembling efforts at talking about Jesus with people, the Spirit is silently at work to interpret, convince, and persuade, because that is what Advocates do.

It is not a bad sign, but a very good one, if things seem to turn out contrary to our requests. Just as it is not a good sign if everything turns out favorably for our requests. –Martin Luther, commenting on Romans 8:26

A DEEP SIGH

We do not know how to pray as we ought, but that very Spirit intercedes with sighs too deep for words (Romans 8:22-27; v. 26).

Sometimes, if we only say one or two words, a friend or a spouse can understand what is on our minds. When we pray, even if we are only able to mumble a few words or phrases inarticulately, the Spirit immediately knows our hearts and gives perfect expression to what we can only vaguely sense. It is all the more reason to "pray without ceasing."

JESUS IS LORD
We ourselves have the first fruits of the Spirit (Romans 8:22-27; v. 23).
The presence of God's Spirit gives us the ability to say "Jesus is Lord." If we have already experienced the joy of believing, we can be sure there are more joys to come, in the power of the Spirit.

INFINITE LOVE
God so loved the world . . . (John 3:1-17; v. 16).
Here is where amazement begins. If we are impressed with the wonder of created life, now our jaws drop in astonishment to consider that God has loved the world through the death of God's Son. If God is infinite in scope and imagination, the death of God's Son "so that the world might be saved through him" reveals an infinite love. Heaven and earth, and the beings that surround the Throne, join with the Holy Spirit urging us to believe in Jesus Christ, the only Son of God.

BORN AGAIN: PART I
". . . born from above" (John 3:1-17; v. 3).
The play on words in Greek is well known—the word *anothen* can mean 'from above' or 'anew', or 'again'. Being 'born again' happens 'from above.' God's Spirit descends mightily upon us at Baptism and captures us for eternity with Christ. Throughout our lives day by day, from above and again and again, we are forgiven, restored, upheld, lifted up to newness of life. Every day is a day to 'repent and believe in the gospel.'

BORN AGAIN: PART II
Jesus answered him, "No one can see the kingdom of God without being born from above" (John 3:1-17; v. 3).
In these verses Jesus speaks both of "entering" the kingdom as well as "seeing" the kingdom. The signs of God's activity in the world are not visible to all. Nor is the way of life to which God calls us immediately self-evident. But when we are born "from above, anew," God's Spirit opens our eyes to see the power of God

63

revealed in the cross of Christ, and to see the way of life that belongs to the followers of Jesus.

LIGHTNING AND THUNDER
The voice of the LORD is over the waters; the God of glory thunders (Psalm 29; v. 3).

When clouds darken the sky and lightning flashes and thunder rolls, there is nothing to do but be quiet and observe everything with awe and reverence. God will get our attention—sometimes with a quiet voice, and sometimes with window rattling thunder. When God gets our attention, we join all in the temple who breathe an awe-struck "Glory!"

A SENSE OF THE HOLY
This has touched your lips, your guilt has departed (Isaiah 6:1-8; v. 7).

There were plenty of "smells and bells" for Isaiah in the temple that day. Awe-struck, his worship gave him a profound sense of the holy. The temple filled with smoke and the prophet felt a hot coal pressed against his lips. "Your guilt has departed!" Faith senses in bread and wine the Lord of hosts coming to us with a purging fire. Your guilt has departed.

NO LIFE WITHOUT DEATH
If by the Spirit you put to death the deeds of the body, you will live (Romans 8:12-17; v. 13).

Before the Spirit can give us new life in Christ the old must die. We cannot have both. Old habits, attitudes, thoughts and behaviors need to be drowned in baptismal water. We cannot remain in slavery and move through the Red Sea to freedom at the same time. The new life entails giving up the old and leaving it behind. "You can't take it with you."

CHILDREN OF GOD
. . . it is that very Spirit bearing witness with our spirit that we are children of God (Romans 8:12-17; v. 16).

The Holy Spirit comforts us beyond measure. Not only does the Spirit take our deepest and most incoherent thoughts and turn them into perfectly articulate prayers in conformity with the will of God, but in our distress the Spirit speaks to the depths of our heart to convince us that, through Jesus Christ, we really and truly are children of God, and there is a place for us in our Father's house.

CAUGHT IN THE ACT

"Where are you?" (Genesis 3:8-15; v. 9).

The footsteps of God, then the voice of God, and suddenly a sensation of dread pulses through our body. God has found us. God has found out! God asks a question to which God already knows the answer. Since we have been caught in the act, the nearness of God is perceived as a threat. God's ultimate purpose, however, is not to scare or punish or threaten. God's ultimate purpose, revealed through Jesus Christ, is to rescue us from our foolishness, embrace us and love us forever.

LIFE OVER DEATH

. . . the one who raised Jesus . . . will raise us also (2 Corinthians 4:13-15; v. 14).

In the resurrection of Jesus God affirms the goodness of creation, making life prevail over death, and corporeality over the nebulous uncertainties of *Sheol*. We cannot imagine what a resurrection body might look like—perhaps as the seed is to the flower, so the mortal body is to the resurrection body—but the promise is resurrection to eternal life through Jesus Christ.

COURAGE TO WAIT

I wait for the LORD . . . more than watchmen for the morning (Psalm 130; vv. 5-6).

If there is danger, let it not be during the night time. Against danger the morning light brings comfort and relief. With even greater intensity than those waiting for the dawn we look for God to reveal the universal glory of the Lord Jesus Christ. It is the promise of the day of the Lord Jesus that gives us courage to wait and hope and trust that 'day is coming soon!'

THE AGING PROCESS
. . . our inner nature is being renewed day by day (2 Corinthians 4:16-5:1; v. 16).

If there is anything positive to say about the aging process, for Christians it is not "aging" but a continual "renewal" in the power of the Holy Spirit. It happens day by day, the Apostle tells us. The Spirit mediates the grace of God for forgiveness, and for strength to forgive, and grace to endure, and grace to understand and love our neighbor. Day by day we learn to live by this grace, and in our weakness we find that "When I am weak, then I am strong" (2 Corinthians 12:10).

A BIG FAMILY
. . . whoever does the will of God is my brother and sister and mother (Mark 3:31-35; v. 35).

The Holy Family of Jesus is bigger and wider than we might have thought. People who may not even be Christians are often engaged in impressive works of charity. The will of God is first of all to believe in Jesus, the One God has sent. The One God has sent told the story of a certain outsider, a 'good' Samaritan. "Go and do likewise," says the One whom God sent.

"We do not build the kingdom of God on earth by our own efforts . . . the most we can do, through genuine prayer, is to make as much room as possible in ourselves and in the world, for the Kingdom of God, so that its energies can go to work."
–Hans Urs von Balthasar (1905-1988)

GROWING THE KINGDOM
". . . if someone would scatter seed on the ground . . ." (Mark 4:26-34; v. 26).

Imagine scattering seed not knowing if rain would come, and no garden hose handy if it didn't. Imagine dropping the name of Jesus on the hard, parched earth of this world where forgiveness is only for weaklings and where acceptance is based on perceived worthiness. Behold! If God can grow the kingdom in our hearts, God can grow the kingdom anywhere. Let the seed of the gospel of Jesus drop, even on hard ground, and let God make it grow.

THE PATIENT GARDENER

"The kingdom of God . . . would sprout and grow, he does not know how" (Mark 4:26-34; vv. 26-27).

Gardeners need to be both industrious and patient. The seed needs to be planted and cared for. Once the seed is in the ground, however, there is nothing a gardener can do to force germination, or growth. A little water helps, but the gardener cannot force the seed to cooperate. We plant the seeds. We give our witness. Then the kingdom of God, powered by the Holy Spirit, will take over from there. The trusting gardener will leave the results in God's hands.

ONLY GOD KNOWS

". . . the seed would sprout and grow, he does not know how" (Mark 4:26-34; v. 27).

The secret belongs to God. We would like to manipulate the process somehow to speed it along. How do people come to faith in Christ? How, exactly, do people who have wandered around the church all their lives suddenly understand the meaning of grace? Only God knows. It is not likely that our experience can be replicated in another's life. We can only give glory to God who miraculously brought us to life in Christ.

A TINY SEED

". . . the kingdom of God . . . is like the smallest of all the seeds on earth" (Mark 4:26-34; v. 31).

The gospel of our Lord Jesus Christ turns everything upside down. Sinners are justified. The leader is a servant. Those who give away receive. And the tiniest seed will bring down the power of sin and evil. God's rule is often hard to discern in the events unfolding in the world. The grace of the Lord Jesus quietly forgives and reconciles. Growing unseen amidst all the other plants, suddenly it comes fully into view, bringing blessing to God's world.

A PURPOSE IN LIFE
And he died for all, so that those who live might live no longer for themselves, but for him who died and was raised for them" (2 Corinthians 5:15-17; v. 15).

Some spend years looking for the purpose and meaning of life. They search for it in what they have or desire to have. Some connect their identity with their vocation. Some find meaning vicariously through what others do. The claim of the gospel is that our purpose for living is to glorify the Lord Jesus Christ in all we do. It is the Christ-centered life, expressed in our words and deeds, that we are looking for.

MATURING UNTIL THE END
In old age they still produce fruit (Psalm 92; v. 14).

How sad it is to meet up with grumpy old people, and how joyful and blessed it is to discover the graciousness of Christ in a person full of years. How sad to go through life—70 or 80 years!—without knowing the peace of God through Jesus Christ. Those who are planted in the house of the Lord are watered by the gospel and the fruits of the Spirit keep on blossoming and maturing, right until the end.

NOT THE CLOTHES
"Your faith has made you well; go in peace" Mark 5:21-43; v. 34).

"If I but touch his clothes, I will be made well." It was not the clothes that the woman believed in but the body inside the clothes. All the fullness and power of God are in Jesus Christ, flesh and blood. Believe in the Incarnation! The fullness, power and presence of Jesus are in the bread and wine, not because it is bread and wine but because that is where Jesus promised to be. "This is my body."

A TRAGEDY
"Do not fear; only believe" (Mark 5:35-43; v. 36).

Even with much faith, a tragedy remains a tragedy, even when Christians are directly affected. When Jesus raised Jairus' daughter we caught a glimpse of the future, a clear manifestation of God's will for us all. While we pray "Thy kingdom come" we live on this side of the cross, supported in the power of the resurrection. Cross before glory always, but in the face of tragedy the glory of the risen Lord drives away fear and instills hope and trust in God's ultimate purpose for us.

CONTRADICTING COMMON SENSE

They laughed at him (Mark 5:21-43; v. 40).

They did not laugh because Jesus told a joke, but because he contradicted common sense. "The child is sleeping," he said, when every scientific test would indicate the girl was dead. Our faith is about life and death, sin and grace. These are serious matters, but when they are conditioned by the words of Jesus, they result in "amazement" (v. 42).

JOY IN THE MORNING

Weeping may linger for the night, but joy comes in the morning (Psalm 30; v. 5).

If we are able to accept it, it is just exactly in the pains of ordinary human life that we experience the solidarity of God. In Christ God comes to save us, but not, strangely, by fleeing from pain and suffering and sadness. God saves us by entering with us into human reality on the cross. It is the resurrection that brings the joy of the morning. Sin, death and evil thus are decisively dealt with rather than merely avoided. By faith in Christ the joy of the morning is ours even in our weeping.

PETER AND PAUL

Let no one boast about human leaders . . . whether Paul or Apollos or Cephas [Peter] . . . *you belong to Christ* (1 Corinthians 3:16-23; vv. 22-23).

If a day is named in honor of luminaries like Peter or Paul (June 29) it is simply to give God thanks for their lives and witness. We have come to know the grace of God in Christ Jesus through the work of innumerable people, living and dead. We pray that God will use our own lives as instruments of blessing for others as well.

PENTECOST

FAITHFULNESS

His mercies are new every morning (Lamentations 3:22-33; v. 23).
The grace of our Lord Jesus comes also in the evening, or at midday, or whenever we need it most. This is the faithfulness of God. We, however, need the rising sun to remind us of God's grace. We need the calendar to bring us to worship. Our faithfulness needs to be continually brought to mind and renewed. God's faithfulness to us in Jesus Christ is always in place and always new.

TRUE WEALTH

Our Lord Jesus . . . became poor, so that by his poverty you might become rich (2 Corinthians 8:7-15; v. 9).
We should not think that faith in Christ will turn into profit. The impoverishment Paul talks about is the Incarnation—when the Son of God became a human being. Jesus became like us so that we might be like God (2 Corinthians 3:18). To know God, to see the world as it really is and everyone in it as God does—this is true wealth, accessible to all through faith in Christ.

SKEPTICAL RELIGIOUS CULTURE

He was amazed at their unbelief (Mark 6:1-13; v. 6).
There was a report of a Lutheran pastor in Denmark who was suspended for saying he does not believe in God. Unbelief may be the result of a skeptical religious culture, but it is nothing new. The people in Jesus' hometown believed in God; they just didn't believe in the reality of God's power to heal and transform lives. Many religious people, accustomed to being "in church" and hearing "God talk," may appreciate the form of godliness while denying its power (2 Timothy 3:5). Through faith in Jesus Christ the power of God for healing and transformation becomes real.

70

A TOUGH SELL

So they went out and proclaimed that all should repent (Mark 6:1-13; v. 12).

So much for advertising schemes that rely on flattery! For those who recognize their need of God the gospel finds eager acceptance. It is a tougher sell for those who are convinced of their essential goodness. If Jesus began his ministry by saying, "Repent and believe in the good news" (Mark 1:14), it is where (gulp!) the disciples of Jesus will also begin. Let us be quick to point out that the call to repent always occurs in the context of forgiveness in Jesus' Name.

ASKING FOR PRAYERS

They cast out many demons, and anointed with oil many who were sick and cured them (Mark 6:1-13; v. 13).

In the Bible one purpose of anointing with olive oil was to consecrate a person to the Lord. By anointing "many who were sick" the disciples showed that the people suffering were special in God's eyes and that God's loving purpose for them was health and wholeness. All who have need of any kind should feel free to ask for the prayers of the church (James 5:14). God's will is to forgive our sins and heal our brokenness, for Jesus Christ's sake.

BY GRACE THROUGH FAITH

. . . to keep me from being too elated, a thorn was given to me in the flesh . . . (2 Corinthians 12:2-10; v. 7).

"God gives everything by grace," Luther used to say. If we are proud of spiritual experiences that come our way, it becomes a hindrance to grace. "The exceptional character of the revelations" does not take the place of living by grace. Even if we all had special visions it would not change the fundamental nature of our relationship with God—by grace through faith in Christ.

PRAYING LIKE PAUL

Three times I appealed to the Lord (2 Corinthians 12:2-10; v. 8).

Paul was the original 'prayer warrior.' Even though Paul prayed 'without ceasing' (1 Thessalonians 5:17), he did not get the answer he was looking for. 'Praying like Paul,' as the song goes, means to keep on praying until God's answer is more important than our desire. In prayer we reveal our mind to God, and in prayer we learn the mind and will of God for us.

NEEDY PEOPLE

My grace is sufficient for you, for my power is made perfect in weakness (2 Corinthians 12:2-10; v. 9).

To live by grace is to acknowledge our weakness. If we claim grace it is because we are needy: we need forgiveness, we need strength for the present and hope for the future. To live by grace is to give up claims of self-sufficiency and let God be the all-sufficient power and strength for our lives. We pray for strength, power, healing; what we get is the sufficiency of grace.

PARADOX

. . . whenever I am weak then I am strong (2 Corinthians 2:2-10; v. 10). Happy are those who have grasped the essential paradox of the gospel. They will not wear themselves out trying to prove their value, strength, or merit. God is able to do wonders just exactly where we are weakest and most ineffective. When we acknowledge sin, God makes us righteous. When we are helpless through illness or unfortunate circumstance, it is the grace of the Lord Jesus that brings wholeness to our brokenness. When our hopes and dreams lie in shambles, the resurrection of Jesus brings life out of our despair.

YOU ARE MINE

Blessed be God . . . he has chosen us in Christ . . . (Ephesians 1:3-14; vv. 3-4).

If our salvation depends on our choosing God we may be in trouble because our natural inclination is to run from God. The good news is that God has chosen us, "before the foundation of the world." When we choose to ignore God or run from God, what turns us around and brings us back is God's long arm insistently tapping us on the shoulder. You are mine!

A LIFE OF HOLINESS
God . . . chose us in Christ . . . to be blameless and holy . . . in love (Ephesians 1:3-14; v. 4).

First there was love. The call to be blameless and holy is also a gift. In Christ God has made us blameless and holy. In love God sees our predicament—afflicted and beset by temptation, taking missteps into the mire, sloshing around, getting stuck deeper and deeper. In love God decided to make us blameless and holy, by the blood of Jesus Christ. To know that we were chosen for this life of holiness is also to know the love of God.

AN OPEN SECRET
God . . . has made known to us the mystery . . . to gather up all things in [Christ] . . . (Ephesians 1:3-14; vv. 9-10).

The mystery is now an open secret. God's purpose is known to us, and we are to make it still more widely known. God's will is to gather all people into the grace of the Lord Jesus Christ. In Christ we are chosen, blessed, made children of God, redeemed from sin and death, called to live holy lives in love for God and neighbor. God wants this for us, and for all people.

MANY DIRECTIONS
[God] has made known to us . . . a plan for the fullness of time, to gather up all things . . . in Christ (Ephesians 1:3-14; vv. 9-10).

The cares of this world, career progress, unrealized dreams, the search for 'God's will' for our lives, drive us in many directions all at once. God's plan is to gather up everything in Jesus Christ, including our own lives, our hopes and dreams. "In Christ there is a new creation" (2 Corinthians 5:17). If we dare to find ourselves in Christ everything else will fall into place. What is worthwhile will happen and the rest will be drained away.

MARKED
. . . you also . . . were marked with the seal of the Holy Spirit (Ephesians 1:3-14; v. 13).

People write their names in books they purchase and even etch their identifying mark on valuable things they own, just in case someone should walk off with something that is not theirs. We should not doubt for a moment that God has put his mark on us. It is a seal that can be read from the inside looking out, or from the outside looking in. 'Child of God, the Holy Spirit is upon you and gives you saving faith in Jesus Christ!'

SUNDAY AND MONDAY

. . . for the praise of his glory (Ephesians 1:3-14; v. 14).

The separation between Sunday worship and Monday service has come to an end. Worship praises the glory of God in Jesus Christ. Day by day God's people, filled with the Spirit, use hands and minds and voice to serve the neighbor in Jesus' Name. When we "do everything in the name of the Lord Jesus" (Colossians 3:17), the Lord's Day praise goes on and on resounding in every Christian's life every day.

RETREAT

"Come away . . . and rest a while" (Mark 6:30-34; v. 31).

"Relatively healthy seniors who pray or meditate may add years to their lives," according to *USA Today*. Jesus already knew that, and so invited his disciples to go on retreat with him. The Sabbath is our weekly retreat into God's word, and in the midst of every day restlessness we need a mini-sabbath as well. St. Augustine said, "Our hearts are restless till they find their rest in thee."

ERASED LINES

. . . brought near by the blood of Christ. For he is our peace . . . (Ephesians 2:11-22; vv. 13-14).

Whatever dividing lines might exist naturally are erased when we profess faith in Christ. If we claim to be righteous before God for Jesus' sake, we claim this righteousness for others as well. Antagonists no more, we are persons whom Christ, in his fleshly death, has made one.

NEARNESS AND DISTANCE

. . . peace . . . peace . . . peace . . . (Ephesians 2:11-22; vv. 14, 15, 17).

Of all the ways to describe our Lord Jesus, here is one more. Christ is our Peace. He is our peace with God the Father and our peace with one another. If we have judged ourselves to be near or far from God, if we have judged the nearness or distance of others from God, Jesus Christ brings all together, binding us up in his love, becoming our Peace. In the process he negates all other judgments. In Christ no one is far off.

DOING NOTHING

He makes me lie down in green pastures (Psalm 23; v. 2).

The roofers, who had been working since sunup and would be hammering away until sunset, were gathered under the shade of a tree, taking a break, for the moment, doing nothing! Life is busy, strenuous, and the sun is merciless. The Good Shepherd commands us to lie down, to do nothing except to be refreshed by his presence and protection. In the cares of today and in the uncertainty of the future, in your need for forgiveness and power over sin, the Lord Jesus orders you to feel the cool, soft comfort of the grass.

WHICH WAY?

He leads me in right paths (Psalm 23; v. 3).

"When you come to a fork in the road, take it," said the Yankee sage. Choices can be agonizing. Even praying about it does not always help, unless we have already decided before we pray. We make a choice and hope for the best. But what if it's the wrong choice? We have a Good Shepherd just exactly because we sometimes do make the wrong choice. The Good Shepherd is there to bring us back and set us on the right path again, and again.

ANOINTING

. . . you anoint my head with oil (Psalm 23; v.5).

In ancient times the oil of olives was used as a cosmetic, especially on festive occasions. In modern times the healing qualities of olive oil are being rediscovered. Oil was also used religiously as a way of consecrating people for service to God. In this beloved psalm we join the poet in expressing amazement for this gift. In the anointing there is both consecration and healing. Jesus is called "Christ", which is the Greek word for 'the anointed One'. In Christ, we too experience the favor and blessing of God.

STREAMS OF MERCY
Surely goodness and mercy will follow me . . . (Psalm 23; v. 6).
However dark the valley, however heavy the burden, we are not alone. Jesus, the Good Shepherd, leads and guides, protects and nurtures. And through it all, we find that we are urged on and encouraged by the ever-flowing streams of goodness and mercy that the Shepherd himself supplies.

THE SOLUTION
He said this to test them (John 6:1-14; v. 6).
The test is knowing where to look for the help we need. There is a large crowd of hungry people. Surely the solution lies over there, beyond our reach, and beyond our means. Or does it? It is always Jesus who asks the question, and it is always a test of our trust and faithfulness. When Jesus is standing at our side can the solution ever be far away?

MEASURING THE RESOURCES
There is a boy here who has five barley loaves and two fish (John 6:1-14; v. 9).
The resources that God gives us are always enough. We are great economists when we measure the need over against what we have, and we let our arithmetic discourage us. We work with what we have. We would always like more resources, more people, more experts to help us. Five barley loaves and two fish were sufficient for five thousand people in God's economy. If we offer up to God's service what we have, meager though it may be, it will be more than enough. God has given each one of us an array of spiritual gifts for the work of God's people. In the hands of Jesus is it always "far more than we can ask or imagine" (Ephesians 3:20).

THE BREAD OF LIFE
. . . they were satisfied (John 6:1-14; v. 12).
There they are, on the highways, and in the malls, and in every new restaurant that opens. Large crowds, anxiously needing something, and always more. In the face of a great need and scarce resources,

Jesus tells everyone to sit down! Be still! Give thanks! And he passes among them, distributing the bread of life to each one. They are satisfied, and there are even leftovers.

LEFTOVERS
"Gather up the fragments" (John 6:1-14; v. 12).
We make jokes about the need or not of praying over leftovers. Leftovers are especially holy, signs of God's abundance and the promise of daily bread for tomorrow. In fact, we should probably give additional thanks and pray more fervently over the leftovers as signs of God's desire than nothing he has created be lost. Even a little bit of thanksgiving for God's benefits is multiplied in powerful ways, as Jesus shows us as we sit on the grass by the Sea of Galilee.

THE FIRST THOUGHT
The eyes of all look to you . . . (Psalm 145:10-21; v. 15).
Perhaps it would be more accurate to say, 'the eyes of all look to the table,' or 'to the refrigerator.' The psalmist teaches us to look first to God in our hunger, pain, or other need. Prayer is not an afterthought, but a first thought. In the acuteness of the moment we turn our eyes to God and discover that God's hands are open, and that God will deal kindly and justly with us. By faith we allow God to inform us of our needs, and to supply them.

PART WAY INTO THE PRESENCE
The LORD is near to all who call on him, to all who call on him in truth (Psalm 145:10-21; v. 18).
We do not judge the sincerity of other people's prayers, but we can judge the sincerity of our own prayers. Sometimes we only manage to come part way into God's presence because the desires of our heart are not in accord with God's will. The "in truth" of our prayers begins deep within.

PENTECOST
SOMEWHERE DEEP WITHIN

I pray that . . . you may be strengthened in your inner being with power (Ephesians 3:14-21; v. 16).

Everything starts deep within, in the inner being. Good thoughts or bad thoughts, good intentions or bad: it all comes from somewhere deep within us. If we are to change our lives and behavior, it will begin with a change in the inner being. The prayer of the church for you and for me is that God will take control of our inner being and sanctify it for the purpose of Jesus Christ.

THE GUEST

I pray . . . that Christ may dwell in your hearts (Ephesians 3:14-21; v. 17).

It is not so hard, after all. We say, "Jesus, come!" and we discover the Guest has been with us all along, and we didn't know it. There are no secret mechanics involved. It is simply to recognize the reality of Christ's Presence. We count on it; we believe it. Christ in our hearts carries us through all the seasons of our lives.

UNFAILING LOVE

I pray . . . to know the love of Christ . . . and to be filled (Ephesians 3:14-21; v. 19).

If you feel a sadness for any person who is unable to experience the love of Jesus Christ, then you are ready to be an evangelist. What a release it is of pent up hurts and grudges, of bad feelings and tormenting memories when the Spirit finally convinces us of the absolute and unfailing love of Jesus Christ! The love of Jesus floods heart and soul, and the broken pieces of our lives are swept away. The love of God in Jesus Christ is never partial. It always fills us up.

LIMITED HORIZON

[God] is able to accomplish far more than all we can ask or imagine (Ephesians 3:14-21; v. 20).

Our requests of God are always too small and never sufficiently imaginative. It doesn't matter because God is more generous than we could ever dare to hope for. Even if we ask for the wrong things, God sees beyond our limited horizon to give us what we really need. God is able from our mistakes, and even from tragedies that befall us, to reshape events and circumstances for our good (Romans 8:28). "Pray without ceasing."

SOMETHING TO CHEW ON

Jesus said to them, "I am the bread of life" (John 6:25-35; v. 35). Do you like the fluffy bread that is mostly air, or do you prefer the kind that requires a commitment before you are able to swallow? There are desires, dreams, obsessions that we pursue with single minded purpose, but in the end they deceive and turn out to be empty and worthless. Jesus is bread, the kind you have to chew on. Take your time. He has given himself totally to you, for your life.

"When I feed the poor they call me a saint. When I ask why people are poor, they call me a Communist"
--Archbishop Dom Hélder Câmara (1909-1999)

STANDING IN THE BREAD LINE

"I am the bread of life. Whoever comes to me will never be hungry" (John 6:24-35; v. 35).
There are many things we "seek after"—a good job, healthy relationships, leisure, security. We strive to obtain these good things as well, perhaps, as things that are not so good. As important as the good things are, they do not, in themselves, "give life." If we are willing to give up the pursuit of other things to stand in the bread line to be fed by Jesus, we will receive "life" and "all these things as well" (Matthew 6:33).

JESUS CHRIST THE PRIORITY

"Do not work for the food that perishes, but for the food that endures for eternal life, which the Son of Man will give you" (John 6:25-35; v. 27).
Daily bread is so important that Jesus taught us to pray for it. In the same way ministry to the hungry is always a Christian concern. As necessary as food is to our existence, even more important is our relationship with Jesus Christ, who gives the bread that "endures for eternal life." Let the priority be our relationship to the Savior, and we will trust God for the perishable daily bread.

NOT COMPLICATED
"This is the work of God, that you believe in him whom he has sent" (John 6:24-35; v. 29).
There are Christians who have gone through emotional experiences and come out with a profound sense of God's love for them in Jesus Christ. Sometimes they may refer to this experience as "getting saved." Other Christians cannot point to anything extraordinary that occurred in their lives: they just know that they have always had faith in Christ, for as long as they can remember. These may feel a little left out of the conversation if they are surrounded by people who "got saved." Experiences, whether dramatic or mundane, will not be repeated from person to person. Salvation is not something to be "gotten," or acquired; it is always a gift, by grace through faith in the Lord Jesus Christ.

MANNA AND THE TRUE BREAD
". . . the true bread from heaven . . ." (John 6:24-35; v. 32).
We, too, eat manna in the wilderness. It is not only the food on the table but everything else we need "for this body and life," as the *Catechism* teaches. All of this, like manna, is temporary. It serves the need of the moment. This manna God distributes liberally to believer and pagan alike. To know Christ is to know the true Bread. The grace of the Lord Jesus brings life into a world that is slowly dying by its own hands.

BREAD OF ANGELS
Mortals ate the bread of angels (Psalm 78:23-29; v. 25).
If a substance scraped off "the face of the wilderness" is the bread of angels, how much more heavenly is the sumptuous feast on our tables several times a day! We are encouraged to "pray without ceasing" (1 Thessalonians 5:17). Especially at mealtime we give hearty, grateful and reverent thanks for what is on the table, much or little, fresh or warmed up. It is the bread of angels, from the hand of God.

PENTECOST

TOUCHING IS BETTER

"I am the living bread . . . whoever eats of this bread will live forever . . . the bread that I will give . . . is my flesh" (John 6:41-51; v. 51).

Even when love is assumed, or taken for granted, it is always better, more comforting to actually hear the words, "I love you." It's even better when there is a hug to go with it. In, with and under the bread of Holy Communion is the "bread for the life of the world." Jesus touches us, God's love is made real. How do I know I will live forever? "The body of Christ, given for you."

NO PITY

Get up and eat, otherwise the journey will be too much for you (1 Kings 19:4-8; v. 5).

"Oh, the Christian life *so* hard! There are so few around us who share our values. If we talk about 'Jesus' they dismiss us as weird religious fanatics." The angel of the Lord has no pity. Of course it's hard! It always has been and always will be. Quit feeling sorry for yourself. Get up and eat! Christ is your bread for the journey.

A DYNAMIC LIFE

The angel of the Lord came a second time . . . "Get up and eat, otherwise the journey will be too much for you (1 Kings 19:4-8; v. 7).

When Jesus says, "Follow me," he calls us to a life that is dynamic, moving, flowing. Even if we would rather just sit still and talk endlessly about 'grace,' or even if we are tired or our feet hurt, we are urged on. There are people to serve, a witness to be made, difficulties to bear with Christian fortitude. But look! Here is food for the journey: the body and blood of our Lord, his Word, the power and presence of the Holy Spirit. Take it all in and savor it, because the journey goes on.

TASTING THE GOODNESS

Taste and see that the LORD is good (Psalm 34; v. 8).

There is something indescribable about faith in Jesus. We can talk about "peace and joy" and other things we experience in the gospel, but these things only become clear and meaningful when

81

we have "tasted" the goodness of the Lord. Taste and see. You might have to change your diet, giving up things that do not feed your soul in order to trust Jesus Christ to pour meaning and purpose into your life. You will see what is meant by the goodness of the Lord.

DRASTIC CHANGES
Thieves must stop stealing (Ephesians 4:25-5:2; v. 28).
What a change faith in Christ brings to the lives of believers! Feeding on the Bread of Life, there are drastic changes in behavior. In the power of the Spirit we are able to "put away" the former things that were obstacles in our relationship with God and with each other. In the power of the gospel, thieves do honest work, gossips mind their own business, and those who nurse grievances learn to forgive. All due to the Bread of Life with which we are fed.

THE NEW SPEECH
So that your words may give grace . . . (Ephesians 4:15-5:2; v. 29).
Part of growing up into Christ involves learning how to speak graciously. Words can hurt, even if we are just kidding. Ridicule is easy, but it is a characteristic of Old Adam/Eve. In Christ, transformed and motivated by the experience of grace, we give encouragement, comfort, and appreciation without treacle or hypocrisy. These mark the speech of the New Creation as we build each other up in the grace of the Lord Jesus.

PASSING BY
. . . be kind to one another . . . as God in Christ has forgiven you (Ephesians 4:25-5:2; v. 32).
A construction worker was hastening back to his work station, passing by co-workers without stopping to chat. His supervisor told him, "You can't just walk by people. It's going to be a long winter." Absorbed in our own concerns, we tend to pass by without noticing the other. We have learned to claim our individual rights at the expense of relinquishing opportunities for service. In Christ, God takes note of everything, and deals kindly with us. It is for that reason the Apostle says, "Be kind to one another."

PUTTING ANGER AWAY

. . . be imitators of God . . . (Ephesians 4:25-5:2; v. 1).

It sounds more than a little presumptuous to think that we could *act like God*! Forgiving one another, putting anger and slander on the shelf, being kindhearted, speaking graciously even when we are perturbed—are these really within our reach? We have both seen it and experienced it. In Jesus Christ God forgives us, sets aside his wrath, speaks kindly and graciously to us. And more: Christ gave himself up to death for the love of the world. It is the same grace of the Lord Jesus at work in us that empowers the Christ-like life.

SETTING SELF-INTEREST ASIDE

Christ . . . gave himself up for us . . . (Ephesians 4:25-5:2; v. 2).

One false god that bewitches our culture is the notion of self-fulfillment. Of course God wants us to be doing things that are fulfilling. But is it possible to find fulfillment in doing things we don't *like* to do? When self-interest is set aside for the sake of loving a neighbor in need, Jesus Christ fills the space vacated by self-centeredness. In Christ even tasks we wouldn't normally *like* to do become fulfilling.

PENTECOST

V. Still Pentecost

THE THREE REFUGES

With all my heart
I take refuge in
God Most High,
Who created all things, the
Merciful Father,
Source of all goodness.

With all my heart
I take refuge in Christ,
The Redeemer from sin,
Who restores my true nature,
The perfect and mysterious
Word.

With all my heart
I take refuge in the One
Who embraces the universe;
Who at all times
And in all places
Responds to our needs,
The pure and tranquil
Holy Spirit.

The Three Refuges composed around 1925
By Dr. Karl Ludvig Reichelt,
Found of Tao Fong Shan Christian Centre,
Hong Kong

THE HOLY CROSS

We proclaim Christ crucified, a stumbling block . . . and foolishness . . . and the wisdom of God (1 Corinthians 1:18-24; v. 23).

Salvation through the cross of Jesus will always seem absurd to the human mind and will always disappoint those who want an early solution to their problems. Only faith perceives that in the weakness and foolishness of the cross the wisdom and power of God become a present reality.

CLAIM THE JOY

. . . be filled with the Spirit (Ephesians 5:15-20; v. 18).

For the human desire for joy and happiness there is an alternative to getting "drunk with wine." When God's Spirit fills us, onlookers might mistakenly accuse us of "being filled with new wine" (Acts 2:15) as on the Day of Pentecost. The Spirit comes without our bidding, but the Spirit's power can be accessed "as you sing psalms and hymns and spiritual songs . . ." Even those who say they cannot sing claim the same power and joy in repeating gracious words of Scripture, prayers and praise.

THE HEARTBEAT OF GOD

. . . sing psalms and hymns and spiritual songs . . . (Ephesians 5:15-20; v. 19).

Singing does make it easier. Even if you don't know all the words, sing the words you do know and hum or whistle or make up the rest. Singing will put you in touch with God's Spirit, and whether it is joy or sorrow that is in your heart, the Spirit will sweep you into the redeeming embrace of Christ our Lord. "Music is the heartbeat of God" –John Ylvisaker.

WISDOM FROM GOD

Come, eat my bread and drink the wine . . . (Proverbs 9:1-6; v. 5).

Jesus is the "wisdom from God" (1 Corinthians 1:30). "You are what you eat is true especially for Christians who gather around the sacred meal of Christ's body and blood. The Wisdom of God Incarnate is wisdom that is imparted to us in the eating and drinking. It is the wisdom of servanthood rather than self-aggrandizement; of self-offering rather than power-seeking supremacy; it is forgiveness rather than vengeance. Eat this bread and the Christ-likeness becomes more and more evident.

FLESH AND BLOOD: PART I

"Unless you eat the flesh of the Son of Man and drink his blood, you have no life in you" (John 6:51-58; v. 53).

We teach that Holy Communion "is the true body and blood of our Lord Jesus Christ under the bread and wine, given to us Christians to eat and to drink."* You are what you eat, and you aren't what you don't eat. If you want to be Christ-like let Christ feed you with his crucified and risen body.

---

*Luther's "Small Catechism," in *The Book of Concord*, Theodore G. Tappert, ed. © 1959 Fortress Press. P. 351.

FLESH AND BLOOD: PART II

"Those who eat my flesh and drink my blood . . . I will raise them up on the last day" (John 6:51-58; v. 54).

Holy Communion is forward looking. Not only are we assured of forgiveness, but our attention is directed to the Banquet of that Great Day of Resurrection when Christ is All in All and we are bound up in the totality of Christ's victory of love and joy.

A TURNING

To those without sense, [Wisdom] *says, "You that are simple, turn in here!"* (Proverbs 9:1-6; v. 4).

People who have awakened to the realization that their lives have not pleased God also realize, painfully, that by their disobedience they have made fools of themselves. To those who desire a strong sense of where they are going, the writer says, "Wisdom" invites you to "turn in here." We now know that Jesus Christ is "the wisdom from God" (1 Corinthians 1:24).

P<small>URSUIT OF</small> P<small>EACE</small>: P<small>ART</small> I
*Which of you desires . . . many days to enjoy good . . . seek peace,
and pursue it* (Psalm 34:9-14; vv.12, 14).
We all want a long life. If we remembered how short life really is,
we might make better use of each day that comes our way. The
psalmist helps us to put content into our lives. "Seek peace, and
pursue it." Jesus wept over a city that did not recognize the things
that make for peace (Luke 19:41). Filled with the Bread of Life,
Jesus is our peace, and teaches us how to pursue it for the life of
the world.

P<small>URSUIT OF</small> P<small>EACE</small>: P<small>ART</small> II
Depart from evil, and do good; seek peace, and pursue it (Psalm
34:9-14; v. 14).
Our faith in Christ is about change. In Baptism, what belongs to
Old Adam/Eve is drowned, so that a new creation can emerge in
Christ. If you are trying to change a destructive behavior, be sure
not only to "turn from evil", but also to "do good." Not only is it a
good idea to refrain from using harsh words with someone, but it
is helpful to praise, encourage, or at the very least offer a kind word
as well.

P<small>URSUIT OF</small> P<small>EACE</small>: P<small>ART</small> III
. . . seek peace, and pursue it (Psalm 34:9-14; v. 14).
Here is advice for people who want the many days God gives us to
be filled with good, rather than merely living many days. As time
goes by we are more and more aware of *how long* people, tribes,
races, and nations can hold a grudge. Filling the many days of
one's life with alienation is surely to relinquish any claim to enjoy
the good. God's gift to us in Jesus Christ is to live without barriers
of hostility. We might as well embrace the gift, and pursue peace
with our closest enemy.

P<small>URSUIT OF</small> P<small>EACE</small>: P<small>ART</small> IV
Turn from evil and do good; seek peace and pursue it (Psalm 34:9-
14; v. 14).
In a game, if the winning team does not press the advantage, they
will be in danger of being overtaken. In the Christian life, wherein

we are freed from sin and its power over us to control and condemn, if we lay back and simply bask in the glow of grace, evil is likely to overtake us once again. The psalmist reminds us of our agenda as people redeemed by the blood of Jesus Christ: turn from evil, do good, pursue peace in every aspect of our lives here on earth.

So Close

". . . among you are some who do not believe" (John 6:56-69; v. 64). This 'Bread of Life' chapter draws to a close on an ominous note. Among even the disciples there is unbelief. "Are you offended" by this talk of "flesh and blood" and "manna and the true bread"? Jesus will always give offense, for different reasons. Here it is the absolute closeness of Jesus Christ to his people that offends. What shocks is the stark sacramental reality of flesh and blood. Jesus' flesh and blood on our lips and in our stomachs! If Jesus were at arm's length it would not be so challenging, but his Body and Blood come close, so close they become a part of us, so that he abides in us and we in him. "The body of Christ, given for you" is answered by "Amen; so be it; let it be to me according to your word; I believe. Amen!"

Where Would I Go?

Many of his disciples turned back (John 6:56-69; v. 66).

In many worship services we eagerly await the reading from the Holy Gospel as we sing, "Lord, to whom shall we go? You have the words of eternal life" (v. 68). This is the answer of faithful disciples when our Lord asks, "Do you also wish to go away?" The call of Jesus Christ to faithful discipleship is renewed each day. Each day there are challenges to our faith. Each day with Simon Peter we say, "To whom shall we go, if not to you, Lord Jesus?"

Choices: Part I

Choose . . . whether the gods your ancestors served ... or the gods of the Amorites . . . (Joshua 24:14-18; v. 15).

The possibility of choosing arises only after we have rejected the God who raised us to a new life in Christ. It is Christ who has first chosen us (John 15:16). If we are unwilling to serve our Lord Jesus

Christ, then we must choose between various other gods—the gods of our ancestors (marauding Vikings or rampaging Goths, maybe!) or the gods of our neighbors. What makes the gospel such overpowering good news is that Christ has chosen us.

CHOICES: PART II

. . . *choose this day whom you will serve* . . . (Joshua 24:14-18; v. 15).

These days it is all about choices. Criminals are said to have made "bad choices." The server in the restaurant will encourage the diner by saying, "Good choice!" Joshua calls the people of God to make a choice. Consider the choices made by those who have gone before, and the consequences, for good or ill. Like Simon Peter, we will cry, "Lord, to whom can we go? You have the words of eternal life."

CRUSHED IN SPIRIT

The LORD is near to the brokenhearted, and saves the crushed in spirit (Psalm 34:15-22; v. 18).

All it takes is one person with a contrary attitude to disrupt your plans and bring your desires to an end. We spend much of our life searching through the brokenness, trying to piece things back together. This is where we will find our Lord and Savior, Jesus Christ. He has been crushed with us, on the cross, and he makes us share in the power of his resurrection.

TOUGHER BATTLES

Our struggle is not against enemies of blood and flesh (Ephesians 6:10-20; v. 12).

The struggle against self-indulgence is real, but there are larger and tougher battles to wage against evil. Demonic forces are seen in social and economic systems that pit clan against clan and class against class, even religion against religion. We could even zoom in closer if we dared. The struggle is against more than human peculiarities. The victory of Christ, however, has turned it into a hopeful struggle whose outcome is already known by faith.

WE ARE CHRISTIANS
Stand therefore . . . (Ephesians 6:10-20; v. 14).
Enough of wishy-washiness! We are Christians! We believe that God has revealed himself in Jesus of Nazareth, his death and resurrection. We believe, because the Spirit has been poured into our hearts. In spite of the disdain or disinterest of neighbor, and in spite of our own reluctance, we follow Jesus in the way of the cross, in the light of the resurrection, believing the words of Jesus that those who lose their life in the gospel will find it.

THE SOURCE AND ENGINE
Pray in the Spirit at all times (Ephesians 6:10-20; v. 18).
Prayer is daunting work when we think it is our work. In another place (Romans 8) the Apostle says the Spirit helps us to pray! Let us not make prayer harder than it needs to be. Let the Holy Spirit be the source and engine of our prayers. "Come, Holy Spirit, pray in me and for me. Here are my concerns, my hopes, my needs, my joys!" You will find a phrase from a Scripture verse will come to mind; the Spirit will put a song on your lips. Prayer is only hard when we forget the Spirit is praying with us.

WHO, INDEED?
Who may dwell on your holy hill? (Psalm 15; v. 1).
This question always alarms us. Who, after all, can say they 'walk blamelessly'? So 'the law is holy, and the commandment is just and good' (Romans 7:12) and if the law shows me my sin it has fulfilled its function. I know my need and the gospel points me to Jesus Christ who becomes my righteousness. In the power of the Lord Jesus to forgive and renew, the fear of the law is gone and the just requirement of the law becomes my goal and delight.

THE MIND OF CHRIST: PART I

"For it is from within, from the human heart, that evil intentions come . . . these evil things . . . defile a person" (Mark 7:21-23; passim).

It all begins in the heart. Just as an athlete might train arms and legs in a set of skills, or as one trains one's fingers to strike the right keys at the right time on the piano, so the mind needs to be trained to think thoughts that will glorify God. When we have the "mind of Christ" (Philippians 2), our actions will reveal the life of Christ that dwells in us.

THE MIND OF CHRIST: PART II

". . . it is from within . . . that evil intentions come . . ." (Mark 7:21-23; passim).

Spiritual power is at work within us, cooking up good or ill. An evil spirit encourages envy, slander, pride, etc., while the Holy Spirit releases us from the oppression of these thoughts, replacing them with the mind of Christ. With the mind of Christ our neighbor is no longer someone to be contended with but someone to be concerned about. "Create in me a clean heart, O God, and put a new and right spirit within me" (Psalm 51).

THE MIND OF CHRIST: PART III

". . . from within . . . from the human heart" (Mark 7:21-23; passim).

Only the very brave dare look deep into their hearts. Open it slowly; one never knows what will pop out! Jesus here recites a catalog of ugly characteristics that have been known to take up residence in human hearts. Sometimes we are amazed at what other people are capable of, only upon reflection to say, "There but for the grace of God go I."

A LITTLE BIT UNCOMFORTABLE

. . . the things that your eyes have seen . . . make them known to your children and your children's children (Deuteronomy 4:1-2, 6-9; v. 9).

Of all the statutes and ordinances laid down by Moses the hardest one might be the command to 'make these things known' to children and children's children. For some reason, actually talking about our faith with family members makes us a little bit uncomfortable. We're not sure what to say. The place to begin, of course, is always with God and what God has done. Where have you seen the grace of God in your life? Still stumped? Did you feel led by God to bring your child to the baptismal font to be made a member of the body of Christ and raised to newness of life? Now you have something to talk about.

"Many people take children into their arms, but few pray for them. If we have contact with children in the spirit of prayer and bless them with our whole hearts, the children will grow up to be great persons." —Toyohiko Kagawa (1888-1960)

ANGER
. . . anger does not produce God's righteousness (James 1:17-27; v. 20).
There is plenty of anger around. Some of it is even righteous anger on behalf of victims of injustice. We want justice, but human justice will always be approximate. God's righteousness is revealed in the cross of Christ where the Son of God takes away the sin of the world. We will be indignant at injustice and take up the burden of the victims, but desire for revenge will not bring God's justice closer. The righteousness of God teaches us to release our anger into the cross of Christ.

REMEMBERING THE IMAGE
If any are hearers of the word and not doers, they are like those who look at themselves in a mirror; . . . they forget what they look like (James 1:17-27; vv. 23-24).
The mirror shows us what we look like. The baptismal font gives us our reflection as well. If we look into the water the image we see is of a person who has died with Christ, been raised with him to newness of life (Romans 6), one in whom the Spirit of God now dwells so that finally it is the image of Christ reflected back in the baptismal water. So soon we forget who we are. It is a daily challenge to connect the hearing with the doing. Beginning our day by recalling the baptismal words, "In the Name of the Father and

of the Son and of the Holy Spirit," will help us remember what we look like in Christ, so that hearing the word we may also be doing the word.

A NICE ARAMAIC WORD

"Ephphatha . . . Be opened!" (Mark 7:24-37; v. 34).
Here is a nice Aramaic word (the language Jesus spoke) to bring to mind every time we open the Bible or listen to the Word of God as it is read to us or preached. Jesus commands the ears of our mind to be opened to what the Spirit is saying to us and to the church. Ephphatha! The Lord God is speaking to us. The whole world is speaking to us, with cries of need and cries of joy. When our ears are opened, it is Jesus, God's Word made flesh, speaking. Tongues also are released, to bear witness.

JESUS IS IN COMMAND

"Ephphatha! . . . Be opened!" (Mark 7:24-37; v. 34).
This is the cry and will of Jesus for all who are bound in any way. God does not will handicap or misfortune, nor bondage to addiction nor slavery to anger or resentment, nor any other condition that limits our true humanity. Jesus is in command of our affliction and by his word the old is sloughed off like a cocoon. Sometimes, when the "thorn in the flesh" seems not to have been removed, we know there is a difference between cure and healing. The final healing is the resurrection, when Jesus will command even our graves: "Ephphatha! Be opened! Rise up!"

FAITH AND WORKS: PART I

. . . so mercy triumphs over judgment . . . So faith by itself, if it has no works, is dead (James 2:1-17; vv. 13, 17).
It is easier to be harsh and judgmental than kind and sympathetic. It is easier to be resentful and bitter than understanding and forgiving. Our faith in Christ gives us a new and different viewpoint. We have received mercy rather than condemnation. For those who have known the triumph of mercy in their own lives through faith in Jesus Christ, the work of faith is kindness, compassion, and mercy.

94

FAITH AND WORKS: PART II
Faith by itself, if it has no works, is dead (James 2:14-17; v. 17).
The sun without sunlight would be a contradiction in terms. If we really believe that Christ has freed us from sin, the sunlight will shine through in real works of love and mercy Otherwise, our profession of faith, however carefully formulated, would amount to nothing more than a glob of gas in the cosmic darkness.

FAITH AND WORKS: PART III
If you show partiality, you . . . are convicted by the law. . . . So faith by itself, if it has no works, is dead (James 2:1-17; vv. 9, 17).
Some people are more attractive than others. This is normal. In Christ, however, we are not normal. We have been transformed and renewed. In Christ, all people—whether they dress nicely or not; whether they are sweetly perfumed or not; whether they are dunderheads or not—are equally important and valued. The work of faith is to love all people, just as Christ loved us.

INAUGURATION DAY
Do not put your trust in princes, in mortals, in whom there is no help (Psalm 146; v. 3).
We pray for our leaders, that their actions may result in the common good. Our "trust", however, is in God. The princes and princesses who hold public office are no different from any of us—they deal with their weaknesses and failures just as we struggle with ours. Therefore, our trust is in God who in Jesus Christ, redeems us from our foolishness.

DO NOT BE AFRAID
Say to those who are of a fearful heart, 'Be strong, do not fear!' (Isaiah 35:4-7; v. 4).
To our friends and neighbors concerned about the 'terrorist threat level,' we boldly say, "Do not be afraid." Our God has come, in Jesus Christ, to save from sin and every danger. In Christ eyes that see enemies are opened to see fellow human beings. Ears are opened to hear the stories of suffering and hopes for a peaceful future. God's vengeance is not against people but against evil. In Jesus, evil has been overcome There is no reason to fear.

HIGH VISIBILITY
He could not escape notice . . . (Mark 7:24-37; v. 24).
The power and presence of God became visible in Jesus of Nazareth. Even the "Syrophoenician" woman, an outsider to Jesus' own people, knew that Jesus was the source of her hope. Our witness is emboldened when we realize that Jesus, not we ourselves, is the attraction. The power and presence of God in Jesus Christ is in our midst as well. It is impossible not to take notice.

NOT TOO PROUD TO BEG
"Sir, even the dogs . . . eat the children's crumbs" . . . "You may go—the demon has left your daughter" (Mark 7:24-37; vv. 28-29).
The Gentile woman of Syrophoenician origin was not too proud to beg. Her need was deep, and she knew where to get help. She asked for a crumb, and was given a banquet. When we lay aside any notion of merit and come before God bringing only our deep need, God's grace is poured out to us in richest measure through Christ our Lord.

UNREBELLIOUS SERVANT
The Lord GOD has opened my ear, and I was not rebellious. I did not turn backward (Isaiah 50:4-9; v. 5).
The words of Isaiah's mysterious 'Servant' are finally fulfilled in Jesus Christ. There are few among us who can honestly say we were not rebellious against God. The strange thing is that the more rebellious we are the unhappier we become. Stranger, maybe, and even more mysterious, is that the Unrebellious Servant of the Lord, Jesus, by his death and resurrection, restores in us the joy of God's salvation.

MISSING THE BEST PART
"Who do people say that I am?" (Mark 8:27-38; v. 27).
Even non-believers like Jesus. The world generally concedes that Jesus was a good person, kind and compassionate. What people don't say about Jesus is more revealing. People who admire Jesus often miss the part of his teaching about the cross. That the power

96

of evil is defeated in the weakness of the cross of Jesus Christ is a message that disinterests many but "for us who are being saved, it is the power of God" (1 Corinthians 1:18).

ABSOLUTE TRUST

"The Son of Man must undergo great suffering" (Mark 8:27-38; v. 31).

It is hard to imagine Jesus with a schedule or a Daily Planner. Jesus lived from moment to moment trusting absolutely the graciousness and goodness of God. The only "plan" was that it would all come together in Jerusalem, on Calvary. Victory through defeat, glory through humiliation, life through death. This is God's secret, too wonderful to keep from talking about it.

ONE WHO SHARES ALL THINGS

O LORD, I pray, save my life! (Psalm 116:1-8; v. 4).

Death, *Sheol*, anguish and distress close in on us from every angle. Surprisingly, this is where our prayers are clearly heard, for the One who shares all things with us, including the depths of despair, is none other than the Christ, the Anointed One, the Son of God, who also lifts us up in the power of his resurrection.

PLAIN SPEECH

He said all this quite openly (Mark 8:27-38; v. 32).

If we, like the disciples, do not always understand Jesus' parables clearly, we cannot miss the point about the cross, since Jesus did not speak obscurely but "quite openly." It is the message we understand but, like Peter, don't want to hear. We want grandeur, glory and comfort for our Messiah, so we can share in it. Instead, we have the cross. Day by day we cry, "O Lord, I pray, save my life!" In the midst of the enemies of life, whether illness, distress, or persecution, the Anointed One is with us. There is yet to be revealed the power of his resurrection. Let this be said quite openly.

RADICAL MOVE
"*. . . let them deny themselves*" (Mark 8:27-38; v. 34).

To the question, "What's in it for me?" the answer is: following Jesus means an emptying of everything that claims your attention, love, allegiance and devotion, in order to find your true love and true self in God. Such a radical move is only possible through faith in Christ, by which we are drawn into the power of his death and resurrection. All our ideologies, schemes and pet projects are surrendered, in order that the power of Jesus Christ may bend and shape us into God's new creation.

GETTING A LIFE
"Those who want to save their life will lose it, and those who lose their life for my sake, and for the sake of the gospel, will save it" (Mark 8:27-38; v. 35).

"Get a life!" we say to people we consider "losers." Some people lose their lives in pursuits we might consider a waste of time. Jesus says the way to "get a life" is to lose it, not just for any cause, but for the sake of Jesus himself and the message about Jesus. The Christian life is not observed, but lived.

SAINT MATTHEW
"Why does your teacher eat with tax collectors and sinners?" (Matthew 9:9-13; v. 11). Here is a "why?" question that has a good answer. Jesus associated with sinful people because they needed him. Sin is a sickness, and all sinners need the cure that only Jesus can give. In the cross of Jesus there is pardon for sin, and power to be raised up in newness of life, freed from sin's oppression.

DISJOINTED PRAYER
Hear my prayer, O God; give ear to the words of my mouth (Psalm 54; v. 2). "The words of my mouth" are often incoherent and disjointed. There is a need for God, a need for deliverance that is sometimes hard to put into words. No matter. "The Spirit intercedes for us with sighs too deep for words." The important thing is that we direct our groaning towards God who does, in fact, hear our prayer.

FUSSING

"What were your arguing about on the way?" (Mark 9:30-37; v. 33).

This may be the most embarrassing question that Jesus could pose to us in the Church, or in our home, or in our world. Are we fussing about the right things? What is important, as Christian people in any venue, is our faithfulness to Jesus Christ as servants of one another. Power, strength, greatness are deceptive attributes. God's power is revealed in the apparent weakness of the cross. The cross of Jesus, bearing one another's burdens, is where we will find our strength as well.

THE GREATEST

They were silent, for on the way they had argued with one another who was the greatest (Mark 9:30-37; v. 34).

One of the surprising features of the kingdom of God is that the notion of "the greatest" has no place. Every act of service, every kindness, every gesture of love, every moment of forgiveness reflects the glory of God in Jesus Christ. When we begin to think our contribution is more significant than another's all it takes is a look from Jesus to quell our vain ambition.

GLORY AND HONOR

They had argued . . . who was the greatest" (Mark 9:30-37; v. 34).

We find competition all over the place, even in the church, even in the first group of disciples! Jesus was talking about the cross, and the disciples were worried about their own glory and honor. Jesus is the greatest just exactly because he became the servant of all. In the church first place belongs to the last. Since we are hardly ever satisfied with being last, least and unrecognized, we will find our 'greatness' in being gathered up, like feuding little children, into the arms of Jesus' mercy.

WELCOME, JESUS

"Whoever welcomes me . . . welcomes the one who sent me" Mark 9:30-37; v. 37).

The greatness and glory of God appears in full bloom in Jesus Christ. Jesus brings the God of heaven and earth so near as to be touched by human hands, and, in human arms, to be embraced by the divine. When we welcome Jesus into our hearts and lives we welcome God himself. Moreover, when we pay attention to the last and least among us, we find we are in the Presence of our Lord and Savior Jesus Christ.

OUR CAUSE

. . . to you I have committed my cause (Jeremiah 11:18-20; v. 20). Jeremiah was a true prophet, so he has the right to be a little paranoid about plots and schemes. In this rebellious world God's Word of truth and righteousness always encounters opposition. Taking matters into our own hands against evil often makes things worse. We can commit our cause to God, because we know that God is committed to saving us from every evil through the death and resurrection of Jesus.

OUT OF OUR CONTROL

Surely God is my helper (Psalm 54; v. 4). The moment when we discover how many things are out of our control could drive us to untreatable anxiety. Or, if we make it a moment of absolute trust in God, it will be a time of profound tranquility. We can scarcely begin to comprehend the inter-relation of events and people, the powers of light and darkness. It is too much for us. Nevertheless, "God is my helper." It is, finally, the grace of God in Jesus Christ that will prevail over the evil in the world and the evil in our own lives.

ENVY

"Whoever is not against us is for us" (Mark 9:38-50; v. 40). Christians sometimes are envious of other Christians who belong to thriving and growing churches whose style and traditions are different from ours. Jesus tells us there can never be too many churches or too many witnesses to God's good news for us in Jesus Christ. Whenever and wherever the message of the gospel is proclaimed, there is reason to give thanks and glory to God the Father for his Son Jesus Christ.

HARSH WORDS

"If any of you put a stumbling block before one of these little ones who believe in me, it would be better for you . . . to be thrown into the sea" (Mark 9:38-50; v. 42).

Sometimes Jesus has harsh words for his own followers. Our actions, decisions and behaviors affect the faith of other believers, one way or another. Sometimes we are encouragers, and sometimes we are stumbling blocks. Death by drowning would be a horrible experience, but since it is suggested by Jesus as punishment for causing others to stumble, we take the warning seriously. If we have caused someone to stumble, this warning turns us into "the little ones" who need the protection of Jesus' mercy.

GIVING AN ARM OR A LEG

". . . it is better to enter life lame than to have two feet and to be thrown into hell" (Mark 9:38-50; v. 45).

It is a serious matter to be a 'stumbling block' that jeopardizes the faith of another person. It is also a serious matter if our actions become a stumbling block for our own faith. Jesus uses hyperbole just exactly because these things are important. Life with God or without God can only be talked about in drastic ways. Life with God is priceless, more valuable even than an arm or a leg. It is Jesus who makes life with God possible. For this reason, Jesus is more valuable to us than our own bodies.

THE TASTE OF THE LAW

The law of the LORD is perfect (Psalm 19:7-14; v. 7).

The psalmist says the law of the Lord, the decrees, precepts, commandments and ordinances of the Lord are worth more than gold and are sweeter than honey. Since our lives are not the gold standard, the law of the Lord tastes sour to us rather than sweet. It is the radical transformation in Jesus Christ, the putting to death of Old Adam/Eve through daily remembrance of Baptism and being raised to newness of life that enables us to taste the precepts of the Lord and declare them sweet.

SUFFERING

Are any among you suffering? They should pray (James 5:13-20; v.13).

If Jesus' disciples did not dare to say "Cheer up!" when he was in agony in Gethsemane, why would we say it to a friend who is suffering? If Jesus cried out, "My God, my God!" we should feel free to do so as well. The proper use of God's name, Luther teaches, is to call upon him in every time of need with prayer, praise and thanksgiving. In calling on the name of the Lord Jesus, we will discover that we have a compassionate God who suffers with us and who will see us through the difficult times.

"Sing all. . . . If it is a cross to you, take it up, and you will find it a blessing. . . . Sing lustily and with good courage. Beware of singing as if you were half dead, or half asleep . . . Be no more afraid of your voice now, nor more ashamed of its being heard, than when you sang the songs of Satan."   --John Wesley (1703-1791)

SING A SONG

Are any cheerful? They should sing songs of praise (James 5:13-20; v. 13).

Now we know a good reason for memorizing hymns and spiritual songs! If you are sad, you need a sad song to sing. If you are cheerful, you need a happy song. "Music is the heartbeat of God," says a modern Christian troubadour. If you don't know the words, at least whistle or hum the tune. It is your prayer of praise and thanksgiving.

VI. Even So, Come Lord Jesus

My Lord and my God
Take everything from me
Which prevents me from coming to you.

My Lord and my God,
Give everything to me
Which helps me draw near to you.

My Lord and My God,
Take me away from myself
And give me entirely to you, yourself.

--a German prayer

EFFECTIVE PRAYER

The prayer of the righteous is powerful and effective (James 5:13-20; v. 16).

There are times when we don't feel like praying, and it may be because we don't feel righteous. If we have positioned ourselves far from God, or if we have turned our backs to God, it should not surprise us if prayer seems ineffective. Claim the righteousness of Christ, let his forgiveness drive away your rebellion, and prayer will once again seem natural and easy.

EVEN SO, COME LORD JESUS

MUTUAL CONFESSION

Confess your sins to one another, and pray for one another, so that you may be healed (James 5:13-20; v. 16).

Our sins of commission and omission are more likely to have victims among those to whom we are closest, even in a Christian community. Christian community is always strengthened, not weakened, by mutual confession and forgiveness. It brings healing and cleansing and renewal to the Body of Christ.

MARRIAGE: PART I

They become one flesh (Genesis 2:18-24; v. 9).

The Bible, just as life, is full of examples that do not match the ideal. Abraham had an unusual arrangement. Jacob had two wives and two concubines. David married a bunch of ladies and Solomon had so many they quit counting after a thousand. Nevertheless the witness of Scripture points to the Man and the Woman, male and female, *ish* and *ishshah*, one flesh, together for life. Moses allowed for new beginnings, and sometimes that may be the best way forward. If modern marriage seems precarious, it is all the more reason to pray fervently and lend support and encouragement for husbands and wives, that their life together will be characterized by mutual love and forgiveness.

MARRIAGE: PART II

Some Pharisees came . . . to test [Jesus] (Mark 10:2-16; v. 2).

If you ask a tricky question you might get a tricky answer. When we put God to the test we always end up getting burned. We could "test" Jesus on any aspect of the Law. How much honor is due our parents? Probably more than we can manage. What kind of "information" about our neighbor can be passed on to someone else without transgressing the Law? Probably less than we thought. When we push against the Law, we always feel its weight and burden. In testing Jesus we discover the guilt of our disobedience. The Law shows us our sin and drives us to Christ.

104

MARRIAGE: PART III
Is it lawful for a man to divorce his wife? (Mark 10:2-16; v. 2).
"All things are lawful," but not all things correspond to God's will and purpose. When we separate what God has joined, there is nothing to do but confess that we have fallen short of the glory of God and claim the righteousness of Christ, by grace through faith. Those who have not experienced the trauma and heartache of divorce likewise need not feel any sense of righteousness. If a marriage manages to stay intact for the duration, the partners will acknowledge that it was all by God's grace.

MARRIAGE: PART IV
"What God has joined together, let no one separate" (Mark 10:2-16; v. 9).
Whether it is magistrate or clergy who says, "You are husband and wife," Jesus nevertheless affirms that married couples really are joined by God. It is the rare couple who needs no help in sustaining a marriage. In any difficult moment it might be helpful to know that it is God who has joined them together, wants them to succeed, and offers daily grace and renewal for it to happen.

MARRIAGE: PART V
"What God has joined together, let no one separate" (Mark 10:2-16; v. 9).
Life is tough, and so is marriage. If marriage were easy couples would stay together. It is God's will that husband and wife should be joined in love and honor "until death parts us." When this relationship is threatened, the very present help in the day of trouble that God offers is the gospel of Jesus Christ. In Christ, we discover the capacity to forgive as we have been forgiven; and in Christ we discover strength to bear one another's burdens.

MARRIAGE: PART VI
"Because of your hardness of heart . . ." (Mark 10:2-16; v. 5).
For Jesus, who skipped the weekend seminar on "How to Have a Great Marriage", the problem with marriages that don't work is sclerosis of the heart, or as Jesus called it, "hardness of heart." Marriage begins with a gleam in the eye, but sooner or later it is

sustained by mutual forgiveness and mutual sacrifice. The things that bring a marriage to an end—abuse, addiction, adultery, e.g.— are all symptoms of hardness of heart. The medicine for a hard heart is the grace of the Lord Jesus. "Be kind to one another, *tenderhearted*, forgiving one another as God in Christ has forgiven you" (Ephesians 4:32).

MARRIAGE: PART VII

. . . a man leaves his father and mother and clings to his wife . . . (Genesis 2:18-24; v. 24).

"Here comes the bride . . ." walking down the aisle, accompanied by her father or a male relative. She relinquishes her father's arm and takes the arm of her beloved. Maybe, like so many other things, we have this just exactly backwards. Biblically, it is the *man* who leaves his father and mother and *clings to his wife*, because she is "bone of my bone and flesh of my flesh." The Christian man loves his wife as his own body (Ephesians 5:29) and hangs on for dear life.

RESPONSIBLE CITIZENSHIP

Hate evil and love good, and establish justice in the gate (Amos 5:10-15; v. 15).

The elders and the powerful gather at the city gate to discuss politics and to judge the cause of one against another. Happy the city and nation that love justice, that value equality, giving opportunity to all. Responsible citizenship is a duty and obligation of those who follow the One who said, "Let your light shine" (Matthew 5:16).

WE ARE NOT GOOD

"No one is good but God alone" (Mark 10:17-31; v. 18).

There is no good news in the admonition to "be good." If only God is good, it means we are not good, nor can we achieve goodness. The effort to win God's favor by "being good" will always be counter-productive. We become "good" only by God's grace to us in Jesus Christ. Our eyes are concentrated on Christ who shows his goodness by making us righteous.

ONE THING

"You lack one thing" (Mark 10:17-31; v. 21).

It might be devotion to wealth that we need to let go of, or it might be attachment to some other kind of activity, value, behavior, or attitude. That "one thing" is whatever our hands are wrapped around so tightly that we are unable to grasp God's grace. "Let go, and let God."

TEARFUL EYES

Jesus . . . loved him (Mark 10:17-31; v. 21).

Here we see the heart of God for a world gone made with insatiable appetite for things. The eyes of God are not blazing with anger, but brimming with tears as the world falls in love with itself and its own production, rather than with God. Even if we walk away from the encounter with Jesus, a quick glance over our shoulder will show us Jesus, who looks after us longingly and lovingly, waiting.

NEVER DULL

The word of God is living and active, sharper than any two-edged sword . . . it is able to judge the thoughts and intentions of the heart (Hebrews 4:12-16; v. 12).

It is frustrating to work with a dull knife. God's word is never dull. It cuts away the nonsense and the excuses to reveal the real state of our souls. Let us not neglect or shun the word, for though it stings (Law), it also soothes (Gospel). Jesus is God's Word to us for forgiveness, reconciliation, and life.

THE THRONE OF GRACE: PART I

Let us therefore approach the throne of grace with boldness (Hebrews 4:12-16; v. 16).

Because of Jesus Christ we can approach God without fear. We are ushered into the presence of God by Jesus himself. We are bold to ask for mercy, because of Jesus. We know where to find help in time of need, because of Jesus' own victory. Let us approach boldly, daily, joyfully.

THE THRONE OF GRACE: PART II
Let us therefore approach the throne of grace with boldness (Hebrews 4:12-16; v. 16).
The sharp sword of God's Word could be intimidating. However, it is just exactly when the Word pierces our soul and shows us our sin that we need to approach the throne of grace. God wants—earnestly desires—to bring forgiveness, renewal and transformation into our lives through Jesus Christ. When our sin pushes us away from God the Spirit draws us in, giving us a bold spirit to seek forgiveness before the throne of grace.

THE THRONE OF GRACE: PART III
Let us therefore approach the throne of grace with boldness (Hebrews 4:12-16; v. 16).
At the door opening to the divine Majesty we pause. We check the invitation to verify time and place and above all, our name. We enter. There is glory and beauty and praise and wonder soaring, cascading, doubling and redoubling and, finally, a throne. It is not judgment, but grace. Everything we wanted to forget is forgotten, what we hoped for is a reality, and we are caught up in endless love.

OUR RELEASE
The Son of Man came . . . to give his life a ransom for many (Mark 10:35-45; v. 45).
The resurgence in various parts of the world of old enmities reminds us how dear to us our resentments and bitterness. Even behaviors which we know to be harmful to ourselves or to other people are hard to change. The price of our release from the power of sin is the death of Jesus. Grace is costly.

JUSTICE
But he was wounded for our transgressions, crushed for our iniquities (Isaiah 53:4-12; v. 5).
The world pleads for justice, but here is a case that defies all notions of fairness. Why should God's Suffering Servant be punished for the sins of other people? Don't feel sorry for Jesus. It

is Jesus who feels sorry for us. More than that, it is Jesus who gave his life for the life of the world.

FOR US

He . . . made intercession for the transgressors (Isaiah 53:4-12; v. 12).

God's Righteous One, Jesus Christ, intercedes for the sheep who have gone astray. Wouldn't it be easier for Christ to judge and condemn? The graciousness of Christ is seen in this, that he intercedes for the transgressors. Christ does not want our condemnation. He desires redemption. He wants us to be restored to fellowship with God. Jesus is on our side!

THE PURPOSES OF GOD

When they call to me, I will answer them (Psalm 91:9-16; v. 15).

"Jesus offered up prayers and supplications, with loud cries and tears . . . and was heard" (Hebrews 5:7). He was heard, yet he died, for a purpose which, from the human point of view, could only be dimly understood. We need to be assured that God hears us in our anguish. If the purposes of God are too obscure for us to understand from this side of the cross, we can trust that the graciousness of God is larger than our own suffering.

LOUD PRAYERS

Jesus offered up prayers and supplications, with loud cries and tears . . . (Hebrews 5:1-10; v. 7). People at prayer often sit around a candle, with eyes closed offering their petitions silently or perhaps with muted voices. An individual in the early morning darkness prays silently while trying to keep distracting thoughts at bay. In contrast, Jesus prayed with "loud cries and tears," because prayer, like all communication, is emotional, and hard work besides. When our energy is spent, we wait in silence for God. Jesus' prayers were heard "because of his reverent submission" (v. 7).

EVEN SO, COME LORD JESUS
THE HIDDEN HAND OF GOD
. . . prayers and supplications, with loud cries and tears (Hebrews 5:1-10; v. 7).

No one said discipleship was easy. Even praying to be spared suffering and difficulty does not always bring about the results we desire. Sometimes the answer to prayer is that God stiffens our resolve to be faithful in the face of discouragement, difficulty and disappointment. Our ways are not God's ways, and our thoughts are not God's thoughts. Before we say "Amen" we pray for grace to trust the hidden hand of God.

God is too good to be unkind, and he is too wise to be mistaken. And when we cannot trace his hand, we must trust his heart.
                                        --Charles Spurgeon (1834-1892)

PLACES OF HONOR
. . . one at your right hand and one at your left in your glory . . . (Mark 10:35-45; v. 37).

The honored places, at the left and right of Jesus, were given to two criminals. For the rest of us, there is the wash basin and the towel, signs of the servanthood to which disciples of Jesus are called. In Christ's kingdom and in fellowship with God's people, it is an honor to be able to serve.

COVENANT
The days are surely coming, says the LORD, when I will make a new covenant . . . (Jeremiah 31:31-34; v. 31).

We may lose sight of the fact that the covenant we have always known is "new." What is new is that God does for us what we cannot do for ourselves, namely, fulfill the law and create righteousness. Jesus is the fulfillment of the law, and Jesus is our righteousness. By faith in Christ, we are declared righteous. This is the covenant that is always new, and never loses its shine.

THE MOUNTAINS WILL SHAKE
Therefore, we will not fear (Psalm 46; v. 2)

Fear lurks just below the surface. In anxious times it bursts forth at the slightest provocation. The mountains will shake, but fear and anxiety can be managed if we know what and Whom we believe and trust. If events close in around us that seem to threaten our well-being, God is even closer. Therefore! We will not fear. The antidote to fear is "I believe in God, the Father, Son, and Holy Spirit" who is our very present help.

GOD'S TRUTH

So if the Son makes you free, you will be free indeed (John 8:31-36; v. 36).

Jesus announces freedom to people who didn't know they needed to be set free. The conventional wisdom of the world is tangled up in a series of falsehoods: that we are better than other people and cultures; that 'might makes right'; or the falsehood that allows some to continually become better off at the expense of those they leave behind. Jesus identifies himself with the Truth that makes us free. God's Truth is Christ whose death frees us to be in right relationship with God, and with our neighbors as well.

JUSTIFICATION: PART I

. . . through the law comes the knowledge of sin (Romans 3:19-28; v. 20).

Some embrace the law thinking that their lives neatly coincide with the law's demands. Others turn their backs on the law, claiming that grace trumps all. Without the law there is no need for grace. The function of the law is to show our absolute, dire need for God's grace. Convinced of our need, we turn to Christ where there is forgiveness of sins, freedom from sin's power, and transformation into God's new creation.

JUSTIFICATION: PART II

Since all have sinned . . . they are now justified by his grace as a gift (Romans 3:19-28; vv. 23-24).

It is the sheer giftedness of the gospel that trips us up. There is a tendency to think that 'grace' is the final little boost we need to get over the top. The gospel says justification is all God's work, not ours. Moreover, the 'all' includes people we don't agree with, and people we consider morally inferior to ourselves. Not our goodness, piety, way of life or life style, but God's grace through Jesus Christ that justifies us and makes us right with God.

JUSTIFICATION: PART III

It was to prove that [God] himself is righteous (Romans 3:19-28; v. 26).

Some expect a righteous God to be a God of vengeance, condemnation and punishment. The gospel of Jesus Christ says that God's righteousness is revealed when God makes sinners righteous. It is a human notion, not a divine idea, that righteousness is delivered in judgment. If things are out of kilter in the world, if we do not measure up, God's idea of righteousness is not to punish but to make things right. God does this by grace, on account of the death and resurrection of Christ.

JUSTIFICATION: PART IV

. . . boasting . . . is excluded (Romans 3:19-28; v. 27).

The great temptation for religious people is to boast. What have we done as individual Christians worth bragging about? What have we done as a Christian congregation? We would like to have a long list to show for our faith, and in our brochures we enhance our Christian résumé however we can. "When you give alms," Jesus said, "Don't let your left hand know what your right hand is doing" (Matthew 6:3). If we are to boast about anything, let it be that God has made sinners righteous by grace through faith in Christ.

THAT DAY! PART I

. . . a feast of rich food, a feast of well-aged wines, of rich food filled with marrow . . . (Isaiah 25:6-9; v. 6).

We do not know, nor can we even imagine, what our resurrected body will look like, except that it will be ". . . imperishable . . . raised in glory and power" (1 Corinthians 15). Bodies, whether physical or spiritual, need food. On that day we can look forward to "a feast of rich food," which like our resurrected bodies, is beyond imagination. Let us just suppose it means that all the food that is harmful now will not harm us then! While we wait for That Day, our Lord Jesus gathers us around his own table to feed us with real food, as a foretaste of the "feast of rich food" when "he will swallow up death forever" (v. 7).

THAT DAY! PART II

Jesus began to weep (John 11:32-44; v. 35).

If Jesus can weep, so can you. Jesus wept because his friend Lazarus was dead. "Celebrations of Life" notwithstanding, the harsh reality of death should never be denied. Jesus was sad because Lazarus was DEAD. The life that God created was now a stench in the tomb. When a loved one dies, let the tears flow. Our tears are gathered into God's hand, and God comforts us in our sorrow with the hope and promise of the resurrection, in That Day!

THAT DAY! PART III

"Take away the stone" (John 11:32-44; v. 39).

The absurd command of Jesus shows clearly just how radical and far reaching is God's work for us in Jesus Christ. Even death is conquered! Day by day, the Holy Spirit summons all the baptized to rise with Christ in newness of life, in anticipation of that Final Summons. Take away the stone, and Christ will give you life!

THAT DAY! PART IV

LAZARUS, COME OUT! (John 11:32-44; v. 43).

The trumpet will give a blast, the dead will be startled into awareness, the Lord Jesus Christ will call out our names, and we will be brought, stumbling and rubbing our eyes, into the bright and glorious light of God. Only God is immortal (1 Timothy 6:1), and only Christ has conquered death. Just as God has given us life out of nothingness, and called us from disobedience to faith in Christ, in the same way we look forward to being called from death to life in the glorious resurrection, on That Day!

THAT DAY! PART V

"Unbind him, and let him go" (John 11:32-44; v. 44).

The butterfly emerges from the cocoon and gingerly expands its wings, getting used to the new life, the air, the sunshine, the flowers, and the freedom! When Jesus calls us out of our darkness into his light, freeing us from sin and death, we blink our eyes in disbelief. Then, we marvel that the old strips of cloth that controlled our attitudes and actions unravel and fall to the ground, no longer holding us back.

THAT DAY! PART VI

God . . . will wipe away every tear from their eyes (Revelation 21:1-6; v. 4).

Tear ducts have a physiological purpose, and also an emotional function. Tears help us express the sadness we experience over death, tragedy, or disappointment. Like a mother who caresses her child's tearful face with a tissue, willing to take the child's pain into her own body, so God has come among us, taken the suffering of humanity into himself through the cross of Christ. Now we see it by faith. Then! We shall see that by God's hand there is no more need for tissues.

THAT DAY! PART VII

Death will be no more (Revelation 21:1-6; v. 4).

In the case of prolonged suffering, death can seem to be a blessing. That does not by any means change the reality that death is God's final enemy (1 Corinthians 15:26). We are filled with anticipation to see what God has in mind for us on the other side of death. Getting there can be wearisome and painful, but on the other side is resurrection: no more death, no more dying, no pain crying out for release.

THAT DAY! PART VIII

"See, I am making all things new" (Revelation 21:1-6).

In spite of daily wonderment at the beauty and glory of life, we know in our hearts that things are not yet as they were meant to be. *We* are not yet as God intended us to be. God's promise is for renewal. All things will be made new. We wait with great anticipation to see what that will look like. Every day God is at work in us, renewing us by the Holy Spirit, conforming us to the image of Christ.

RESOURCES: PART I

I have . . . only a handful of meal . . . and a little oil . . . (1 Kings 17:8-16; v. 12).

We do not need to be modest about what we have to offer God. If it seems like nothing, all the better. When we are down to the last handful of flour or our last two copper coins, we are ready to make an offering of biblical proportions. We have no skills or possessions or time that have not been given to us by God. When we give of ourselves, however much or little it seems to us, in faithful obedience to Christ our Lord, it always turns out to be more than enough.

RESOURCES: PART II

I have . . . only a handful . . . (1 Kings 17:8-16; v. 12).

It is true that we underestimate the value of what we have. We have "only" this or we are "only" that, as though the glory and honor derives from who we are and what we can do. If we have little resources, talent or imagination, let us trust that God can take the little and do great things. In that way, pride in what is accomplished is replace by amazement at what God does.

RESOURCES: PART III

. . . only a handful of meal in a jar . . . (1 Kings 17:8-16; v. 12).

If only we had more! If only we were more talented; if only we had more people! If only we had *the right kind* of people! Most of the time we just have to work with what we have, and the people God has put us into fellowship with. It's practice for heaven. It is also a way to be faithful. When we see what needs to be done in service to God or neighbor, let trust in the power of the Lord Jesus drive out fear and timidity. God is able to use the little we have, or are, for God's great purposes. Then let God be praised for the outcome.

RESOURCES: PART IV

The jar of meal was not emptied, neither did the jug of oil fail (1 Kings 17:8-16; v. 16).

We tend to be more comfortable when our cupboards are well stocked and our bank balance hefty, but God does not work that way. Jesus taught us to pray for "daily bread," not for a year's supply at one time. The widow of Zarephath and her household were fed, one day at a time. Each day God's grace is sufficient for the day.

RESOURCES: PART V

"They devour widows' houses . . ." A poor widow came . . . (Mark 12:38-44; v. 40).

There is a contrast here between those who have much and want more, and one who is willing to give up the very little she has. Jesus condemns the one and praises the other. Our thirst for more and more is the desert wind that dries up our faith. Not many can sing *"Take my silver and my gold / Not a mite would I withhold"* with a straight face. "God has chosen the poor to be rich in faith" (James 2:5).

LONG PRAYERS: PART I

"Beware of the scribes, who . . . for the sake of appearance say long prayers" (Mark 12:38-44; vv. 38, 40).

They often ask the pastor to pray, and the pastor obliges by saying the longest prayer he or she can think of, lest the people think they're not getting their money's worth. The best prayers are the heartfelt ones uttered by any Christian where appearance counts for nothing and where simply a desire to be with God is everything.

LONG PRAYERS: PART II

". . . who, for the sake of appearance, say long prayers" (Mark 12:38-44; v.40).

The next time you are visiting a friend in the hospital or are asked to open a meeting with prayer, remember: Jesus does not expect a long prayer! There is nothing wrong with a long prayer if there is much on your heart, but neither is there virtue in a long prayer if you are just repeating yourself or trying to impress someone. Lay before God what is on your heart—your needs and thanksgivings. Then claim your right to do so in Jesus' name, and say "Amen!"

LONG PRAYERS: PART III

"Beware of the scribes . . . who say long prayers . . . " (Mark 12:38-44; v. 40).

There is nothing intrinsically wrong with a long prayer. Jesus himself "spent the night in prayer to God" (Luke 6:12) but this was a private conversation with the Father. The prayer Jesus taught his disciples ("Our Father . . .") is the model of succinctness. "Pray without ceasing" (1 Thessalonians 5:7) admonishes the Apostle, but let prayer be simple, sincere, unadorned with flourishes meant to impress whoever is standing nearby.

"I have never heard a sermon from which I have not derived some good, but there have been some near misses."

--Mark Twain

IN COMMUNITY

. . . not neglecting to meet together, as is the habit of some (Hebrews 10:11-25; v. 25).

Christians are not 'lone rangers.' The branch cannot exist apart from the vine. The arm or leg cannot live separated from the body. A worship service may be exciting or dull, from the human point of view, but the degree of excitement or dullness is really beside the point. When we are "in Christ" we are "in community." When we "meet together" around Word and Sacrament, we, the branches, are nourished in Christ the Vine.

PROVOKING ONE ANOTHER

Let us consider how to provoke one another to love and good deeds, not neglecting to meet together, as is the habit of some (Hebrews 10:11-25; vv.24-25).

The ministry of "love and good deeds" can take place wherever a Christian encounters human need. It can also take place in the gathering of God's people, in worship or in smaller groups. People who "meet together" for Bible study and prayer naturally grow to have concern for each other's welfare. It is a perfect place to "provoke one another to love and good deeds."

117

EVEN SO, COME LORD JESUS

EVENING PRAYER

I bless the LORD . . . in the night also my heart instructs me . . .
Psalm 16; v. 7).

The idea of 'night-life' needs to be reclaimed for the Lord. Somewhere between the agitation of the day's activities, the meetings, the 'going out', the switching off the television, and finally slumber, there is a silent stillness where God desires to encounter us. It may be something as simple as saying Luther's Evening Prayer, or the Lord's Prayer, individually or together as a family. What if we sang a hymn? Then, if sleep proves to be elusive and all you hear is the furnace coming on and off, perhaps God is telling you it's time to pray.

ON OUR BEHALF

Christ . . . entered into heaven itself, now to appear in the presence of God on our behalf (Hebrews 9:24-28; v. 24).

Our great comfort is just exactly that it is Christ the exalted Lord of heaven and earth, the One to whom all authority has been given, who is in heaven *on our behalf!* The focus of our faith, then, is Christ. We do not look to ourselves, or to what we have done. When we say we 'have faith,' we mean that the object and focus of our faith is Jesus Christ.

LIFE, IN FULLEST MEASURE

Christ . . . will appear . . . to save those who are eagerly waiting for him (Hebrews 9:24-28; v. 28).

We believe that history will be brought together in a meaningful way by the appearance of Jesus Christ as Lord of all. We look forward to it, praying earnestly, "Come, Lord Jesus!" because it will be the day of salvation. Sin, evil, death will be destroyed and in its place, justice, peace, gladness, and life in its fullest measure.

THE FOUNDATION

"Do you see these great buildings? Not one stone will be left here upon another; all will be thrown down" (Mark 13:1-8; v. 2).

We admire buildings, especially tall ones. We do our best to protect and preserve old buildings, calling them "historic." If God

118

did not spare the temple in Jerusalem we should not be surprised that other buildings will crumble and fall as well, even church buildings. As strange as it seems to us, God can get along without buildings. The foundation is Jesus Christ. "Like living stones, let yourselves be built into a spiritual house" (1 Peter 2:5).

BEING LED ASTRAY
"Many . . . will lead many astray (Mark 13:1-8; v. 6).
There is no shortage of "end times" scenarios, and all of them exist only to lead us astray! The end of all things is in God's hands, and God's plans are inscrutable. All we know of God and God's will is what has been revealed to us in Jesus Christ. The best counsel is to look to Jesus in all circumstances, asking God's Spirit to help us discern what faithfulness to the Lord Jesus Christ requires of us today.

DAY OF TESTING
. . . those who lead many to righteousness, [shall shine] like the stars forever and ever (Daniel 12:1-3; v. 3).
Those of us who have never experienced persecution may wonder how we would respond in the day of our testing. Hiding from the threat of harm or death would certainly be a temptation, but our calling is always to bear witness. Those who point to Jesus Christ, whatever the cost and whatever the consequences, in this way leading many to righteousness, "shall shine like the stars forever and ever."

GREAT RESISTANCE
". . . the beginning of the birth pangs" (Mark 13:1-8; v. 8).
"Thy kingdom come!" If it were easy for God's kingdom to burst into our world, we would not have to pray for it. As it is, the old world with its injustice, hatred and greed is so appalled by God's kingdom of justice, love and peace that there is great resistance. Nevertheless, God's kingdom will come, and the rumors of war and the upheavals of the earth are signs that it is on the way!

RESURRECTION

Many of those who sleep in the dust of the earth shall awake . . .
(Daniel 12:13; v. 2).

Like a houseful of sleepyheads, slowly rousing themselves one after another, the hope of resurrection begins to emerge in the consciousness of God's people. Resurrection will always be puzzling to Christians and absurd to skeptics. Even today, perhaps especially today, the scientific reality of death makes us skeptical of faith's hope of resurrection. We need not speculate on what or how. We only need to embrace the promise that God's last word is not death but life.

THANKSGIVING

May those who sow in tears reap with shouts of joy (Psalm 126; v. 5).

A Russian Orthodox bishop said, "If you consider yourself to be rich, you have nothing to be thankful for." Thanksgiving comes from the edge of the cliff. Just when we were ready to fall over the precipice, we were saved. The sinners covered by the grace of the Lord Jesus breathe a sigh of relief and rebellion is turned to praise. The anxious cast their burdens on God and find peace. And if there is no job, whatever is on the table is perceived as the richest blessing of God.

THE BASIS OF EVERYTHING

Grace to you and peace (Revelation 1:4-8).

To the exile on Patmos Island and to Christians everywhere in every kind of circumstance, our Lord Jesus brings grace and peace. Even though we use the words 'grace and peace' with almost every breath, the reality behind these words is neither trite nor commonplace. Grace is essential to our relationship with God. It is the most amazing concept of all, because it runs counter to our intuition. God has forgiven us, accepted us, gathered us to his people, with no motivation at all except grace. It is only on account of God's grace that we dare talk about peace, and it is because of grace that we even dare look in God's direction.

THE SON OF MAN

I saw one like a human being ["Son of Man" in the older translation] *. . . And he came to the Ancient One . . . To him was given dominion and glory and kingship* (Daniel 7:13-14).

If we are to choose a Ruler we might choose the strongest, tallest, the one who can talk the loudest. Jesus is presented to the Ancient of Days and given "dominion, glory and kingship," not by virtue of strength but by virtue of obedience, even to death on a cross. The power and glory of God was hidden in the weakness and shame of the cross. Therefore, the Ancient of Days has highly exalted him, and his everlasting dominion over sin, death, and evil shall never be destroyed.

CHRIST THE KING: PART I

What have you done? (John 18:33-37; v. 35).

It seems odd to us that the roles are reversed. Usually it is the judge who tells the accused what the charges are. With Jesus everything is reversed. Sinners are forgiven, the self-righteous condemned. Forgiveness, not vengeance, is the way of life for disciples. Servants are the greatest in Jesus' realm, and kingship for Jesus is obtained by yielding to enemy powers. What have you done? Jesus has rescued us from ourselves.

CHRIST THE KING: PART II

"Everyone who belongs to the truth listens to my voice" (John 18:33-37; v. 37).

Pilate was understandably confused. He had never seen a king without sword or army. Jesus is a king whose sword is God's truth. Jesus himself is God's Truth, and in Jesus all humanity—with our load of hatred, jealousy, warfare, rebellion and unfaithfulness—is taken up into the love of God on the cross of Jesus Christ. By this act of willing self-sacrifice Jesus is exalted and made Lord of all, and our Lord, too. This is the Truth to which we belong.

CHRIST THE KING: PART III

"Everyone who belongs to the truth listens to my voice" John 18:33-37; v. 37).

In this noisy world there is a voice that neither screams nor scolds. Jesus is the voice of God's truth. Jesus leads us away from false worship, false values and ideals, from false promises, and leads us to uncluttered faith and confidence in the love of God for us and for all people. Those who want to distinguish between what is real and what is illusion will listen to Jesus with all seriousness.

CHRIST THE KING: PART IV

Jesus Christ . . . ruler of the kings of the earth (Revelation 1:4-8; v. 5).

It is really a question of ultimate loyalty and identity. Jesus is our Sovereign and we are citizens of the kingdom of God. Other loyalties to nation or institution, to profession or hobby, are secondary and tertiary. In the end, even the kings of the earth, in their pomp and splendor, lay down their banners to do obeisance at the feet of Jesus Christ.

THE FIRST AND THE LAST

"I am the Alpha and the Omega" (Revelation 1:4-8; v. 8).

Before time, the Word was. And at the end, the Word will be. Christ is the beginning and the end, the first and the last, the A and the Z, the East and the West. In our beginning, we were baptized into Christ. We press on, until we reach our end, when our lives are fully conformed to the image of Christ with which we were marked at baptism.

FAMILY DEVOTIONS

"We'll have devotions now," my Dad would say.
With much to do or little on his list,
Around the kitchen table, ev'ry day,
For lack of time God's word would not be missed.
With Bible story book in easy reach
He read it through, and read it twice again
And gave us more than Sunday school could teach
From Genesis to Revelation's end.
We bowed our heads and Father said a prayer,
Devout, heartfelt, unending though, I thought,
Commending all to heav'nly Father's care,
Each named to God and leaving no one out.
   In fam'ly's mealtime talk our lives are normed,
   And there in conversation Christians formed.

--jmf

9 780578 154763